A Place Called Home

A Home for Peter

By Edna Stark

Orange Hat Publishing
www.orangehatpublishing.com - Waukesha, WI

A Place Called Home: A Home for Peter
Copyrighted © 2019 by Edna Stark
ISBN 978-1-64538-053-5
First Edition

A Place Called Home: A Home for Peter
By Edna Stark
Cover Design by Kaeley Dunteman

For information, please contact:

Orange Hat Publishing
www.orangehatpublishing.com
Waukesha, WI

Orange Hat
PUBLISHING

www.orangehatpublishing.com

Dedication

This book is dedicated to all the children who have no parents, or have lost their mother or father in death or other ways as a young child - as Peter had when he was left alone to find his own way in life. He was found with God's help when someone cared enough to help and showed there is always an answer.

I thought of my life as a large family, broken up and put on farms to help with crops while some of us were in orphanages.

I thought about how lucky I would have been to find someone like the Watkins - loving and caring Christians. I learned later in life how God was my protector and watched over all of us. Not just the rich, but also the lost and lonely. I have learned that God is only a prayer away just as Peter learned this as a small boy.

Part 1

Going Home

Peter and his family lived in a small town in Georgia called Rome. A very pleasant town with a small population, but everyone was so friendly and kind.

They lived in a small house that was cold and drafty because there was very little work for the men. Some worked in the coal mines and some as blacksmiths on the railroads. Peter's Dad was a coal miner and wasn't always at home. He died from a disease called Legionnaires'. In those days they had no cure for many diseases, so Mary and her son Peter were alone to watch over each other. They would read the Bible every night before retiring.

One morning they got up to have breakfast together. Mary had gotten Peter ready for school and was about to leave, "Goodbye Son," she said, "I love you!"

"I love you too, Mom ."

She worked long, hard hours and never complained.

One day, Mrs. Glennis was late coming home and Peter began to worry when suddenly the door opened and she called out to Peter.

"Peter!"

Peter ran to the door and saw that a neighbor had brought his mother home.

"She got sick at work, Peter, so I brought her home," said Mrs. Hartel.

"Thank you very much," said Peter.

They got Mary to her bed and covered her up warmly. "I will take care of her now," said Peter.

"I will fix her some hot soup. That will warm her up," said Mrs. Hartel, and she said goodbye to Peter.

His mother finished her soup and fell asleep. Peter stayed with her and did not leave her side all night.

His mother was very weak and was running a high fever. Peter was scared and knelt down to pray that she would get well soon.

The next morning, Peter fixed his mother

some hot tea and hot oatmeal.

"Please eat a little," said Peter. "I will go get the doctor, but you must eat."

Mrs. Glennis had a little tea and oatmeal while Peter went for the doctor.

When they returned, the doctor and his assistant, who was training with him, went in to see Mary and asked Peter to wait outside the room for them.

Moments later they came out and said to Peter, "Son, your mother is very ill, but you are doing a good job taking care of her. Keep her in bed and keep her warm. Give her lots of liquids, and if there are any changes, get a hold of me right away."

Peter answered the doctor. "Thank you! I am glad you could come…"

Peter stayed with his mother at all times and had not gone to school. The doctors checked her again later and there was little change until the following week. Peter was in the kitchen and his mother had called him. "Peter, can you come here?"

"What, mother?" asked Peter.

"Come here," she said softly. "Sit here, son, on my bedside. We need to talk."

Peter's Mom had heard the doctor tell Peter that she wasn't doing well and realized how sick she was. She was worried about her son and began to wonder what Peter would do without her and who would take care of him.

When Peter sat beside his mother, he asked, "What do you want to talk about, Mother? Everything is going to be okay. I can get a job and we can take care of each other. I can take care of you. Don't worry, Mom !"

"Peter," said his mother. "You have to go to school and get an education. Promise me you will go, Peter. Please! That is very important to your Dad and I."

"I promise, Mother," said Peter, "but nothing is going to happen to you. You will get well. I know you will. You rest now and I will be back soon."

Peter made himself something to eat so he could keep his strength up and watch his Mom . When she awoke, she found Peter sitting by her side, holding her hand and crying while talking to God.

His mother said with a soft voice, "I had a message from God last night, Peter. Listen, Son. He gave me a sign that you will be taken good care of by someone very nice if anything happens. Did you hear me, Son? I don't know who they are, but God will know."

"I heard you, Mother, but you will be there to take care of me."

"Peter, my son, you have to be a strong boy. I need you to listen. God loves you and will protect you. Always remember that. So does your father who watches over you."

"But mother!" Tears were running down his cheeks. "I don't want you to go. I can take care of you. Please don't leave me alone. Please, Mother!" He put his arms around her and laid his head upon her, weeping.

Mary soothed Peter and said, "Peter, you must not cry. It will be alright. Now dry your tears. I have never known a more wonderful son, and I am so proud of you, Peter."

"Thanks, Mother, you have been a wonderful Mom . I...I don't want you to go!" he cried.

"That is God's wish, dear. You must not think He is doing this to punish you," she started to say. "God bless you, my son." Her voice became very weak and she spoke with a low murmur, but Peter heard it and repeated the words back to his mother.

"God bless you, too, Mom ."

He ran to Mrs. Hartel's and asked her to call the doctor.

"I think my mother is...is gone."

"What do you mean, Peter?"

Crying hard, Peter told Mrs. Hartel his mother wasn't breathing, and then they both ran over to Peter's house to see Mrs. Glennis.

"Is she...is she...gone?" asked Peter.

"I don't know. We will get the doctor."

When the doctor came, he pronounced Mrs. Glennis deceased and asked the neighbor if she would stay with Peter. She comforted Peter as much as she could and she had tears herself. Mary had been a good friend and neighbor.

Peter was on his own and found life hard and very lonely without his loving mother and no one to watch over him or take care of him. After the funeral, which was small and quiet, the Minister took him home and stayed with him for awhile. As he left, he said to Peter, "You are not alone, son. God is always with you. Remember what your mother taught you and if you need someone to talk to, I am always here to listen." With that he said goodbye and gave Peter a hug.

Peter was alone for the first time to shed the tears he had held back. He asked God to guide him in the way he would want him to go. His neighbor, Mrs. Hartel, who brought Peter's mother home one day, had stopped to see how he was doing.

"How are you, Peter?" she asked.

"I'm scared," said Peter. "I don't know what I am going to do."

"You are going to be okay. You know your Mom was very sick, but she is looking after you and so is God. If I can help you, please come find me. I must go to work now. Take care and God bless you."

As Peter went on with his life, the next few weeks were very lonely and the food was running out, so he went out to find work. He was very unhappy, but he put on a brave front while he was out looking for things he could do to earn money. Neighbors and friends wanted him to stay with them, but he would not leave his mother and Dad's home because it was a place he had grown up in and loved.

He continued looking for jobs for nearly two months, living on what he had left to eat. When Peter ran out of food, he became very weak. He remembered his Mom's last words and cried out loud.

"Oh Mother, why did you leave me? Why?"

He was walking down Main Street, feeling very light headed and weak, when he passed out on the sidewalk in front of the store Lyndin and Murray. There was no one in sight to speak of, and Peter laid there quite a while before anyone found him.

Someone Who Cares

It was about eight o'clock when a tall young man in his late twenties was walking alone with a heavy load on his mind, not noticing anyone or anything until he almost stumbled. He looked down and saw a young boy lying on the sidewalk. He bent down to pick him up and found he was unconscious, and felt for his pulse but it was very faint. So, forgetting his own problems, he picked Peter up and carried him to the City Hospital, which was two and a half blocks away. He had left his car at work because he wanted to walk home.

When he arrived at the hospital, he could see no one around, but then he noticed a light on in one of the offices where there was a nurse standing and said to her, "Are there any doctors here that can help this boy?"

"No, sir, there are no doctors. They are out on calls. Is there something I can do for you?"

The young man introduced himself as Mr. Watkins and said to the nurse, "This little boy has got to have a doctor or he isn't going to last long."

"I am very sorry, but the doctors will not be in 'til the morning."

"Isn't there someone that can look at him and see that he's alright?" asked Mr. Watkins. "He needs care."

"Well, let me see if we have a room for him and when the doctor comes in, we will have them look at the boy," said the nurse.

Mr. Watkins was satisfied with that and took Peter to his room and thanked the nurse.

"Who is he?" she asked.

"I...I don't know. I found him on the street unconscious near the Lyndin and Murray grocery store," Mr. Watkins replied.

"Well, it looks like you need your rest, too, Mr. Watkins," said the nurse.

"I would like to stay a while if I may," replied Mr. Watkins. "He may be frightened when he wakes up."

"Certainly," said the nurse. "If he awakes, please call me."

Mr. Watkins sat beside Peter for an hour, but Peter, still looking feverish and pale, did not stir at all. Mr. Watkins left wondering if his wife was getting worried. He left a message for the nurse or doctor asking them to call him as soon as they knew anything. Then he went home and wondered whose boy he was, where his parents were, and where they lived. All kinds of questions went through his mind, and he was determined to find out. "I have got to find out what the boy's name is."

Mr. Watkins was the manager of the boys Christian home near the town of Rome where he lived for many years and was very well known. He was about 28. He loved children and worked with boys who had family problems. Most of them turned out to be good boys deep down, and learned to care about others.

Peter had learned from his parents to always be kind to others and love everyone, not just his friends. He was kind-hearted and always willing to help anyone in need. Now he needed someone.

When George Watkins got home, it was almost ten o'clock and his wife, Lynda, was still waiting up for him. She met him at the door and gave him a hug.

"What happened? You're so late. I was getting very worried!"

She could tell there was something wrong, so she asked, "What's wrong, George? Did you have a hard day?"

"Yes, dear. I would rather not talk about it right now. It's terrible, some of the things that happen in this world."

"Well...what did happen?" asked Lynda.

He started telling Lynda the story of how he found Peter lying on the sidewalk unconscious and carried him to the hospital. However, he was tired and hungry and just wanted to call it a day. Ready to lie down, he said goodnight to his wife. She watched as he went up the stairs.

In the morning, as they had their coffee and breakfast, George remembered he was expecting a phone call but never got one.

"I am going to the hospital," said George.

"Do you know who he is?" asked Lynda.

"No," said George. "He didn't have any identification on him. He was so weak and was wearing ragged clothes. I felt so sorry for him." Then he turned to Lynda and asked her, "Would you come to the hospital with me? To see the boy? I can't wait for the call."

"Yes, dear, if you want me to. I would be glad to go with you," answered Lynda.

The two of them finished breakfast and were ready to leave, but Mr. Watkins had to first stop at the boys school to check on the boys. Then they were on their way to the hospital to see Peter, whom they knew nothing about.

When they reached the hospital, the nurses were busy giving the patients daily baths. Margaret Lansing, the supervisor of the hospital, was at the desk working on reports when Mr. and Mrs. Watkins walked in with a very unhappy face. She wondered what was wrong.

She asked, "Is there something I can help you with?"

"Yes, my name is George Watkins and this is my wife, Lynda. We came to see a young boy that I brought in last night. We don't know what his name is, but we would like to see him."

"Do you know what room he is in?"

"Oh yes, he was on the second floor in a quiet room," answered Mr. Watkins.

"Alright," said Margaret. "You may go up. There is a nurse at the desk. Just tell her I gave you permission to see the boy."

"Thank you," said the Watkins' and they went up to see Peter.

When they reached Peter's room, he was looking weak and lonesome while lying quietly and looking at the ceiling, not even noticing they had walked in. George touched Peter on the arm softly and Peter turned to see a tall, handsome man looking down at him. He looked very much like he had remembered his father. Then he turned to see Lynda and wondered who they were.

"Who are you?" asked Peter.

"I am Mr. Watkins. This is my wife, Lynda. I found you on the sidewalk unconscious last night and brought you here. What is your name?"

Mr. and Mrs. Watkins saw tears come to the boy's eyes and heard him say, "Love thy neighbor as thyself."

Again, Lynda asked Peter his name and he answered, "My...name is...Peter...Peter Glennis."

"Where are your parents, Peter?"

Peter broke into tears and could not answer.

"The poor child...Peter, did...did you lose your parents?" asked Mr. Watkins.

Peter, still crying, tried to answer. "I didn't lose

them. They will never be lost...God just...took them home with Him."

Peter grew tired and the Watkins said they would be back. They gave Peter a goodbye and left feeling worried and sad about what had happened.

Walking slowly down the hospital hall to the elevator, they wondered what to do next. Margaret, the head nurse, noticed them and asked, "How is the little darling doing?"

"I think he will be okay after he gets rest and some food. I suppose you know his parents are both dead," replied George.

"No...I didn't. How sad! I can see why he is so quiet...he's heartbroken. Does he have any relatives he can live with?"

"I don't know," answered Mr. Watkins. "He was so tired...all he really said was 'Love thy neighbor as thyself.'"

Margaret felt horrible and wondered how something like that could happen to a small, innocent child like Peter.

When George and Lynda left, they told the nurse they would be in later to see Peter.

George took Lynda home and went to the Christian school for boys to see some difficult boys that were just brought in. He caught up with the workers and introduced the new boys to the group they'd be with.

At the end of the work day, he went home and rested awhile before going back to the hospital. Lynda sat in a chair next to George and wanted to ask him a question, but wasn't quite sure how to ask him or if she even should. She wondered if it would upset him to talk about Peter, but maybe he's thinking the same thing, so she decided to ask him. "George, what are we going to do about Peter? He seems like such a good boy."

Sitting up straight, George was startled by Lynda's question because he had been wondering the same thing. "I don't know Lynda, we have to find out if he has any living relatives first. If he hasn't, then...well…" George didn't finish saying what he was thinking.

Lynda then asked, "what will happen to him? Will he go to the boys' school?"

"No," answered George, " I don't think Peter needs to go there. He seems to have Jesus in his heart and believes in him and he knows right from wrong." George and Lynda had tried for some time to have a child of their own, but were not successful.

Peter was just the type of boy they could love and raise as their own. George continued and said, "I thought maybe, that is if you wanted to, we can bring the boy home with us, and if things work out, maybe we could adopt him as our own son?"

"Oh darling, I'm so glad you said it. I was hoping you would, because I know you have become fond of the boy," said Lynda.

"He will be the boy we always wanted."

"Yes," said George, "he does need a home, and with our help we can give it to him."

"You and our son! That will be wonderful George!" said Lynda, as she embraced George.

As they drove to the hospital that night to see Peter, they were quite happy and had very little conversation. When they reached the hospital they saw one of the doctors and asked if the young lad was better, and the doctor replied yes, and said they could go see him. When they got to the room Peter was sleeping. Lynda touched him on the arm lightly and he awoke smiling.

"Hello Son, How do you feel?" said George.

Peter looked up and said, "oh it's you sir. I...I feel a little better, the doctor said I could go home soon, but I...I don't want to go home. I missed a lot of school, too," Peter said, trying to hold back his tears so that George and Lynda wouldn't see.

"Do you have any living relatives?" asked Lynda.

Peter looked at the Watkins and answered, "the only relative I know of is an aunt, and I don't want to live with her because she doesn't like children, so I, I don't have a home to go to except my mother and father's. I love and miss them so much."

"We're glad you love them, and we don't want you to ever forget them," said George.

"I would never do that," said Peter.

"I love them too much to forget them, Mother taught me to pray when I was six years old. She always told me to remember the verse in the Bible."

"Is it the one that says, 'Love thy neighbor as thyself'?" Lynda asked.

"Yes, how did you know? Did you know my parents? They were good Christians and taught me a lot of good things," said Peter.

"No son, we heard you say it when you were alone this morning. We think it's special to remember that."

"Do you teach Sunday school?" Peter asked.

"No, but I teach many boys to get along and to

love and help each other and to love Jesus. This is at a Christian home for boys without parents." replied Mr. Watkins.

Peter sighed a deep sigh and asked, "will I go there? I don't have parents or a place to go."

"Well let's wait and see, where would you like to go Peter?" Asked Mr. Watkins.

"I don't know," Peter answered.

"Well don't worry, we will find you a place to stay. When did the doctor say you could go home?" Asked Mr. Watkins.

"I don't know, he only said I was doing better," answered Peter.

The Watkins told Peter to get some sleep and they would stop by in the morning if he wanted them to. "How does that sound to you Peter?" asked Lynda.

"Oh, yes," answered Peter. "I would be real disappointed if you didn't because I don't know anyone except Mrs. Hartel!"

"Who is she Peter?" asked George.

"She is my neighbor and lives by my house," Peter replied.

"Alright, we will see you tomorrow. Okay get some rest," said George.

"Thank you for coming, when I get home

again, I will come and see you," Peter replied.

"Good," said Lynda, "but you better get some sleep now and get well so you can."

When they left Peter laid thinking how nice they were. His thoughts were interrupted when the nurse came in with his tray and said "Peter, here is some hot soup and ice cream, try to eat this, so you can get strong again! If you need anything, just push this button, okay?"

"Okay," answered Peter. The nurse left and Peter sat up and ate his meal. Then he settled down for the night.

The Adoption

Everyday for a week, George and Lynda visited Peter to see how he was coming along. They were thrilled to see him improving so quickly. He could even stand up and walk without getting dizzy. In that time, Peter grew fond of the young couple. They reminded him of his mother and father: so kind and understanding.

He couldn't help but think about how wonderful it would be if they would let him stay with them, maybe even adopt him. He knew his parents would be more than happy to know what fine people were taking care of him. Finally, the day came when Peter was told that he could go home when there was someone to take care of him and give him a good home. "But I...I don't have anyone, Doctor," said Peter.

Just then, George and Lynda came in. "How is he, doctor?" George asked.

"Well," said the doctor, "he is ready to go home. However, he has no guardian."

"That's not a problem," Lynda said. "We will take him home and see what we can work out."

"Thank you," said the doctor. "I will release him in your care."

The Watkins walked over to Peter and asked, "Why are you crying? You should be happy, the doctor said you can go home."

"But, I...I don't have anyone to go home to," Peter replied and started crying harder. Lynda took him in her arms and tried to comfort him.

"Now, now, Peter. To us, you do have a place to go home to. That is...if you want to?"

Peter wiped the tears from his eyes and asked, "Where? Is it in town near my Mother's house?"

"Yes, it's in town" the Watkins replied. "It's with a couple that you know. It's with us, Peter. Would you like that?"

"Do you mean that? I can go home with you folks? I...I would like that very much." Peter gave them both a big hug and smile. It was the first time he remembered being happy since his Mom had died.

"There are a few things we have to do first, Peter," George said.

"What?" asked Peter.

"Well, first we have to get permission to take you home with us. We also need to get you some clean clothes. You were in pretty bad shape when I found you; so you will have to stay here until we get things in order for you," said George. Peter sighed and laid back on his pillow.

"We will be back to get you," said Lynda. "Don't you worry." They each gave Peter a hug and said goodbye. The nurse came in to check on him and told him to get some rest.

Peter said to the nurse, "Do you have a Bible? My Mother always read it at night with me and it gave us both a peaceful feeling."

"I will look and see. I will be right back," said the nurse.

The nurse returned with a Bible and told Peter he could use it as long as he liked and then she left Peter with a goodnight smile.

Peter awoke the next morning with a fresh day ahead of him. The nurse had brought his breakfast in. She said, "I hear you are going home today. I hope everything goes well for you."

"It will, because God is with me; and when my

Mother was sick, she told me some Christians were going to care for me. She said God sent her this message. She was right."

"I'm glad," said the nurse, "the Watkins are very good people."

The next day, the Watkins came back to the hospital to take Peter home to stay with them. They explained to him, that he would live with them, but they would have to go to court to see if the judge would let them adopt him and if the judge approved the papers, they would have to wait six months.

"But why six months?" asked Peter.

"Because it gives you and us time to get to know each other as a family. It's a test or trial time, Peter."

When the court day for the adoption came, Peter was asked some questions by the judge.

"Peter, do you want to live with the Watkins as your adopted parents?"

Peter had no doubts at all about the Watkins, because they had always been very kind and caring people, and answered "Yes, your honor. They are loving people and they took care of me when I was sick and alone."

"The second question, Peter - how long were

you and your mother alone after your father died?"

"My father died two years ago, and that left my mother and I alone to take care of each other."

"When did your mother die, Peter?"

"She died," Peter started crying, and feeling unhappy he answered the judge, as memories of his mother came to him, "My mother died two months ago."

The judge had heard that Peter had been brought up in a Christian home and had helped others to learn of God's love. The judge and the Watkins felt good about Peter.

"Peter", said the judge, "are there any questions you want to ask before I make my decision?"

Peter answered, "No, your honor, I like the Watkins. They have given me a home and love that I thought I would never find again since my Mom my and Daddy died."

"Well I guess that answers my questions." said the judge.

"Mr. and Mrs. Watkins, would you come up and sign these papers, and then you and your son may go home."

"We would be glad to sign them," said the Watkins'.

After signing the adoption papers, Peter smiled

and looked at the judge and the Watkins and asked, "Does this mean I can live with you forever?"

"Yes, Peter" said Lynda and George

The adoption went through and Peter was now Peter Watkins and not Peter Glennis anymore. But, he never forgot his own mother and father, who had given him life, and love, and the many things God had taught them and about caring for others. But something still bothered Peter, and he said to the judge, "What about my Mom and Dad's house and the things I have there?"

"Well, my boy," the judge answered, "I am sure if you ask your new parents, they will help you with that and you can tell them where it is. Is that okay with you, Peter?"

"If it's okay with them," he replied.

"We will be glad to take you, Peter, and we can take care of the house for you as well, okay?" Mr. Watkins asked.

"Yes, sir. That will be nice. Thank you," said Peter.

After Peter settled into his new home, George and Lynda took him over to his parents' house. It made Peter cry to think that he could never come back except to ride past to keep the memory of his parents alive, although he knew that they would've liked George and Lynda.

When Peter got to the house that he grew up in, he went to his room and knelt down to pray by a picture of his Mom and Dad. He asked God to watch over and protect them. As they left, Mrs. Hartel stopped by and told Peter to come and visit sometime. When Peter said goodbye to his Mom and Dad's house, he took their picture with him, because that was all he needed to remember them by.

"Come on Peter," said George. "Let's go home, okay?"

"Okay, Dad!" said Peter, and he put the picture near his heart to let them know he was okay and that he loved them.

After they returned to his new house, Peter got settled in and got back to school. He had quite a lot of catching up to do, but George and Lynda were happy to help him. This made them proud, because they had always wanted to be able to sit and help their children and to watch them grow up and graduate from college.

Peter liked school and was very intelligent and patient. As he grew up and attended high school, he ran into a subject that he had trouble with. It was Algebra. He knew that he had to pass it to make it to college. He studied hard with his Mom and Dad's help, and when exams came back with good grades, he knew God had helped him through them and he gave thanks for his parents help.

Graduation Day

George and Lynda loved Peter as if he were their own flesh and blood. Peter was as special to them as they were to Peter.

Peter graduated from high school with honors and his parents were very proud of him. They threw him a party, but Peter didn't know about it.

"Dad," said Peter "Mom ! What a nice surprise! How did you do it without me knowing it? Thank you!" And he gave them both a big hug.

His friends all clapped and cheered, "Congratulations, Peter!"

After the crowd left, George and Lynda asked, "Peter what are you going to do now that you are out of school?"

Peter replied, "I thought I could work with you at the school, Dad. Maybe I could help other boys like you helped me."

"I would be happy to have you by my side, Peter. I was hoping you would, but what about college?"

"Well," said Peter "I want to be a minister. I plan to work a couple of years and save tuition and expenses. What do you think of it? I want to talk with both you and Mom before I make up my mind, that's why I want to work with you for awhile."

Lynda was very happy with Peter's decision. They promised to help him through his ministry and be there for him whenever he needed them. The following week was a trying time for Peter, because he visited the school for boys that were hard to get through to, but working with them was going to be even more trying.

Mr. Watkins took him to work for the first time and said to Peter, "Peter, this may seem very unhappy for you at times, but remember that these boys have come from a life of hard knocks and some have a very bitter outlook on life. You will see that they are boys that need someone to listen to them. Do you know what I mean, Peter?"

"Yes Dad," Peter answered.

He continued to tour the school and got to know the area. He watched the students and learned how each one was different.

Peter Joins His Father

Peter joined his father at the boys school where he would work for the summer. As he got to know the school and the boys there, he thought how nice it would be to help another boy come to know God and his willingness to help.

There were two boys about Peter's age when he lost his parents. He had found them very bitter that their parents had left them at the school. Their names were John and Jerry. One day Peter asked the boys what they would like to do when they were out of school.

They both looked at him and John replied, "I don't know." Jerry agreed and said, "Me neither. What can we do, anyway? We can't do anything."

"Well," said Peter, "there are so many things that God has created and so many to help people like yourselves. God has helped me get to know that there are sick, sad, and very lonely people out there. I know because I was one of them. I lost both of my parents, but was lucky to find a family who cared enough to take me in and love me. My parents died when I was about your age. So, you see, you're not alone in this. I was alone for several months after my mother died and had no one to turn to. The Watkins found me unconscious on the sidewalk and gave me a home. My mother told me it would happen before she died."

"But, how did she know?" asked the boys.

Peter answered and said, "God had spoken to her that night. So you see, if you just believe that things are good and listen to God, you will find a piece of tranquility or belonging. Do you know what I mean?" he asked the boys.

"I guess," said the boys, not quite sure of what Peter was talking about.

Peter gave them each a book to read before they went to bed and said, "Read this. I will see you boys tomorrow. We can talk about the book then."

"Okay, Peter," they said. "See you tomorrow."

The boys, as young as they were, wondered about what Peter said, how he lost his parents, and why he wanted to work at the school. They finally fell asleep thinking that maybe they too could find someone who cared enough to teach them the things Peter's Mom had taught him. In the morning the sun shone through the boys' window, and as they awoke John asked Jerry, "How does God make the sun rise so bright? It looks like a ball of fire far away."

"I don't know," Jerry replied. "We can ask Peter or Mr. Watkins. They might know."

"That's a good idea," said John. So they got up, wondering what was going to happen that beautiful Saturday.

Some of the boys had homes to go to, but John and Jerry's parents seldom picked them up to go home for a weekend. "Are you going home, Jerry?" asked John.

"I don't think so...my Dad is always gone and, well, my Mom is...dead. Are you, John?" asked Jerry.

John laughed. "I guess not. My parents say they can't handle me being around. They say that I get into too much trouble all the time and it upsets them. So I stay here and the counselors usually plan things we can do together."

"I hope Peter comes," said Jerry. "He said he would see us today."

As the boys prepared for the day, they went down to breakfast. There were several boys who didn't go home for the weekend. As they gathered to the table, they clasped hands and asked God for blessings. Jerry didn't say a prayer, and the counselor asked him to come to her office when he was done with breakfast. The counselor's name was Martha Blake. When Jerry went into the office to see her, she asked him, "Jerry, why didn't you say your blessings along with the boys for breakfast?"

"Because we never say them at home, so why do I have to say them here?" said Jerry.

"Aren't you thankful that you have a place to stay and food on the table Jerry?"

"Yes Mrs. Blake," he answered. "I don't want to say them" hiding his face as he started crying.

Mrs. Blake didn't know what to say to him. "Will you try next time, Jerry? For me?"

"I'll try." said Jerry, and then asked if Peter was going to come today.

"He will be here this afternoon and will gather with all the boys," said Mrs. Blake.

"Oh good," said Jerry. "He said he would see us and he will. Okay!"

"Do you like Peter?" asked Mrs. Blake.

"Yes, he knows how we feel. He gave us a book to read last night and said that he would see us today" said Jerry.

"Okay, Jerry, you may go join the other boys. I'm glad you like him. He's a very nice leader. I hope he can help you."

"Thank you," said Jerry and went to join the other boys. John saw him coming and went to meet him.

"Are you alright, Jerry?" he asked.

"Yes, Mrs. Blake just wanted to know why I didn't say my blessings with the rest of you at breakfast."

"Well," said John, "why didn't you?"

When John asked Jerry why he didn't say his blessings with the others, Jerry became upset and said, "Because I didn't want to, my Dad never says them. He says there is no God. So why should I say them? I don't believe there is either, so leave me alone" said Jerry.

"Jerry!" said John. "Come on, let's go by the rest of the gang and see what they are doing," trying to change Jerry's mood.

Jerry calmed down and said, "Okay, but I wished Peter was here."

As they joined the others, they began to enjoy

themselves as a group. It was a small group because many of the boys had gone home for the weekend.

"Hello, boys", came a voice that Jerry and John had recognized.

"How is everyone today?"

Some of the boys stood up and said, "Hello, Peter, we're glad you're here. I knew you would come."

"Hi Jerry," said Peter, "I told you I would, didn't I?" He said this with a smile.

"Yes, and John and I have been waiting for you. What are we doing this afternoon?"

"Well, first I have a short meeting and then we will gather in the gym. Is that okay?" asked Peter.

"Yeah!" yelled the group of boys.

Peter met with Martha Blake, the morning counselor, to see what she had for the afternoon.

"We had a young lad that had a problem, Peter, and maybe you're just the one to help him get on the right track."

"What do you mean, Martha?" asked Peter. "Who is this boy?"

"Do you know the boys, Jerry and John, in room 120?" asked Martha.

"I have met them. They seem quite disturbed

boys. Jerry more so than John. Are they brothers?" asked Peter.

"No, just roommates. They get along okay. John seems to be able to help Jerry with his anger and get him to do things that we can't."

"Like what?" asked Peter.

"Many things, like playing together, reading Bible scriptures and others."

Peter seemed quite concerned and asked about Jerry's parents.

"Jerry's Dad is never home and his mother died, and John's parents think he is too much trouble at home. The boys have become friends and they seem to trust you Peter, so I thought maybe you could spend some time with them after the other boys are settled in their rooms."

"I will try and...maybe I can see what causes Jerry not to believe in God," replied Peter.

"Oh, Peter" said Martha, "I called Jerry into my office because he wouldn't say blessings with the others. He didn't tell me why, but said he would for supper. Let me know how he does."

"Yes, Martha. I will talk to him. Thank you for letting me know."

Mrs. Blake picked up her papers for the day and told Peter she would see him on Monday.

Peter said good afternoon to her and checked his schedule for the afternoon then continued on to gather the boys. Being Saturday, Peter had planned on getting acquainted with the boys. As he gathered them together in the gym, he asked each one to introduce themselves and he did the same because he was also new to some of the boys. Then he said to Jerry, "would you like to say the prayer we all say together before starting our afternoon?"

Jerry looked at Peter and said, "No."

"Why, Jerry?" Peter asked.

"Because I don't want to," he said.

"Okay, who would like to say it?" All the other boys raised their hands, so Peter said, 'Well what if we say it together? Will that be okay Jerry?"

Jerry said "Okay" but could not get the words out.

Peter noticed it, but pretended not to, because he didn't want the other boys distracted, thinking in time Jerry would join in. After prayers, Peter asked the boys what they would like to do. A game of basketball or a walk out in God's fresh air to see the nature of his beauty. Since it was such a beautiful day, they decided to go nature hunting and explore God's world. Some boys brought back things they could talk about and others, like Jerry and John, just enjoyed being out. They discussed the joy of seeing different trees and how big God makes them. How the flowers grow in the fields and how God scatters the seeds.

The afternoon passed quickly and the boys had a few minutes to share together their problems. Peter spent time with Jerry, somehow he had to help and bring him to know how God can help him. "Jerry," Peter said, "Can I talk to you alone?"

"Oh...yes" Jerry said.

They walked over to the room off the gym, but Peter could still see the other boys. They sat down together and Jerry had a happy face, just knowing someone cared about him.

He said to Peter, "what do you want to talk about?"

"Well Jerry, Miss Blake tells me you never said prayers at home, is this true?"

"Yes, it's true, my Dad and Mom didn't believe in God and I don't either. Why do you believe in him Peter?"

"Well" Peter said, "Let me tell you a story. There was a very young lad, like you. Who didn't know who God was. Do you Jerry?"

"No, who is God?"

"Well", said Peter "he makes the wind blow, the flowers and trees grow. You saw all the wild flowers in the fields didn't you Jerry?"

"Yes," Jerry said.

"Well how do you think they got there?"

"I don't know," said Jerry.

Peter answered by telling Jerry that God makes the wind spread the seeds and we can't see the wind, but we can feel it. "Can't we?"

"Yes," said Jerry. "But how does he make it?"

"Well because he is God and the creator, he can do anything. He makes it rain to make things grow and sunshine to dry up the rain and a rainbow is his promise that he is here for us."

"What happened to the boy?" asked Jerry.

"Well," said Peter, "His parents read to him out of the bible and taught him that without God and prayer - "

"What is prayer?" interrupted Jerry.

"Well Jerry, prayer is like talking to a good friend and asking for answers or help that you might need, only you talk to God in Heaven. We need to thank God for all he has done for us. That is why we say grace at meals. God gives us all this, he created us in his image, so we are to be kind like he is. Do you understand Jerry?"

"I guess so, but what happened to the boy?"

"Well," Peter said. "This young boy grew up in a good adopted home and loves to help others to understand God. You see, I am that boy. I learned when my Dad and Mom died there was a God and he helped me to grow in him and love my new parents."

"Who are they?" asked Jerry.

"Do you know the Watkins?" asked Peter.

"Sure, are they your adopted parents?"

"Yes," said Peter, "they taught me many things, so you see Jerry there is a God. Will you try to say your prayers next time, okay?"

"I will try," said Jerry.

Peter hugged Jerry and said, "Thank you son, and now we better get the other boys and get ready for supper, okay. Would you help me Jerry?

Peter and Jerry walked together and John walked over to Jerry, "Are you okay?" he asked. "Did you get hollered at?" John asked.

"No! Peter was very nice. I wished my parents and yours were like him."

"Why?" asked John.

"Because I like him, he helps and cares about us."

John was surprised to hear it come from his roommate who so resented anyone who believed in the Lord. They gathered with the other boys and sat down for supper.

"Now who would like to say grace tonight?" asked Peter. Several raised their hands and among them was Jerry. A little afraid and wondered why they were all looking at him, but he didn't back down. Peter said, "okay Jerry," with a smile on his face. Jerry said the prayer and felt proud.

John sat next to him and said, "Jerry what happened? You never say grace."

"I had a good talk with Peter and he said things that no one else has ever talked to me about," said Jerry. "Not even my parents."

"About what?" said John.

"I will tell you tonight in our room," Jerry said.

"Okay," John said and they finished their meal and Peter and the boys went to get in a game of basketball before retiring for the night, As they went to their rooms, Peter told them if there were anyone who wanted to talk he would be in his office and they could feel free to come at any time. The boys looked at each other and walked on.

While back in the Watkin's home, Mr. and Mrs. Watkins sat by the fireplace wondering how Peter was doing. They went on reading the paper and saw an article that took them back to when Mr. Watkins found Peter, and talked about how proud they were of him and would miss him terribly when he goes off to college. He had done so much for the boys. The boys at the school had learned to trust Peter and turned to him for help and counseling with God. Who would they get to take his place, and would they be able to understand them as Peter did? What would Jerry and John do without him there? They must talk to Peter about it when he comes home, so he and Lynda waited up for Peter. Peter got home soon after 11:00 p.m., surprised to see his Mom and Dad waiting up for him.

"Hi Mom and Dad, why are you up so late? Is everything okay?"

Peter was tired, but was never too tired to take time for his Mom and Dad. "It was very rewarding, Dad. I had some good talks today with the boys. We went and explored the outside world and played a game of basketball. But the most rewarding part was...well...do you remember Jerry and John? "

"Yes, how are they?"

"Well," said Peter, "I think I got Jerry to understand more about God. He offered to say grace at supper tonight!"

"Peter! That is wonderful."

"No one has been able to talk to those two boys. How did you do it?" asked George.

"I just talked to Jerry alone for awhile. He said he didn't believe there was a God. Then I told him the story of my life and asked if he knew you. He said yes, so I told them of my story and how God helped me find you and that I always thank God for my blessings. Jerry asked how I knew there was a God, and I told him, you can't see the wind but you can feel it, and there's evidence in the rains that make all things grow and promise in His rainbow. He was amazed and something changed in him. I can really see the change in both of them, Dad. I hope when I go off to college, they will help you with the others. They are fine boys; just had a hard life and no one cared until now. But I think they are going to be okay now. Thanks be to God."

"Peter, we were worried about what was going to happen to them. But now we know," said George.

"They will be alright. Thanks to you, Peter, and God who sent you to us! And to the boys who trust you. They will miss you and so will we, but we are glad you want to be a minister."

"Thanks Dad," said Peter. "If it hadn't been for you and Mom taking me in, I might be in a situation some of those boys are. You know I love you both, do you?"

"Yes, we do," said Lynda and, "we love you too."

As they sat and talked, it was getting late and they were all getting tired and gathered to say a prayer before calling it a night.

"See you in the morning," said Peter and he went upstairs.

"Wait Dad, is there anything special for the boys I should do?"

"No," said George. "They will gather for church at ten o'clock. Reverend Jake Anderson will be there to give the sermon."

"Okay Dad, I will see you in the morning."

On Sunday, Peter went to church early with his Mom and Dad, and then went to the school to be with the boys. When he got there they were all up and ready for breakfast, except one. When Peter got to the boys school wondering where John was.

"Did John go home this morning?" he asked the night person.

"No," said the boys.

"Well where is he?" asked Peter.

"He left some time during the night, and we don't know when or where he went," said Ray the night attendant.

"Why didn't someone call us? George will have to know," said Peter.

Peter asked Ray to stay for a little longer and get the boys ready for breakfast and then church, and he would notify the Watkins. The boys gathered for church and the minister gave the sermon. "Let's pray," he said "for the safety of our friend John."

The sermon for the boys was one they could understand. How parents and children can grow together. Peter called John's parents to see if John had gone there, but was told he hadn't, and then he called George and was concerned about John.

"No! Son, he isn't here, we haven't seen him. I hope nothing has happened to him. I will call the authorities and we will go to the school, okay Peter? It will be okay."

"Has he done this before, Dad?" asked Peter.

"No," said George, "Peter I will be right there, talk to Jerry and see if he knows anything."

"Okay, I will," said Peter. "He had asked the night attendant when he last saw him, and he replied about early morning check time."

"I'm sorry Peter."

"It's not your fault Ray. He will be back I'm sure."

Peter asked Jerry if there was anything bothering John during the night. Jerry took Peter to his and John's room. He showed Peter some of John's pictures of his Mom and Dad. Jerry said, "Peter...John thinks nobody cares about him so he said he was leaving on his own. He said he was going to his grandmother's house in Texas. But Peter, he didn't have any money. How is he getting there?"

"I don't know Jerry," said Peter.

"Jerry, thank you for telling me this. I will go to the bus depot and see if I can find him. Can you tell the boys and Ray that I will be back?"

"Yes," said Jerry.

"Thank you," said Peter.

Peter went to the bus station and did not see John at first, until he saw a boy lying on the bench waiting for the morning bus. He walked over to John and sat down beside him. He put his comforting hand on John's forehead. He felt warm and knew he had to get him back to the school and call the doctor. He picked John up and carried him to the car and drove back to the school. John was cold and hungry. Peter let the authorities know that John was okay, and George was there to help with the other boys. He thanked his Dad for coming on Sunday and staying with the boys. Sunday was quiet after everything settled down, and Ray went home after church so the boys could spend time reading or doing other activities they enjoyed. Peter talked to John and tried to help him understand the trials of life. He told him he could call his grandmother tomorrow, but right now he needed rest.

"Jerry, would you keep John company for a while? Let me know if he needs anything."

"Yes sir," said Jerry.

So John fell asleep while Jerry looked at the book Peter had given them when he first came. At suppertime, all the boys surrounded John and asked questions, but Peter said, "Boys, let's sit down so we can say our prayers together and remember to thank God for safety and that we are glad to have John back, okay?"

John was glad to be back among those who

cared about him.

Sunday was over for Peter, and John and Jerry had helped each other to understand God and how he protects us when we do things we shouldn't do, because we hurt others, not just ourselves.

Peter decided he would stay until morning. If John woke up he would be there for him. He had promised him he could call his grandmother and he would also like to talk to John's parents. Would they come and see John, or even care what their son wants? When Monday arrived and George came to the school, the boys were just arising for breakfast. "Good morning Peter," said George.

"Hi Dad," Peter replied. "How are you and Mom? I am glad you're here. I told John he could call his grandparents today, and I think we need to call his parents together and have a talk with them. What do you think Dad?"

"You're absolutely right. John needs them and he needs to know they care about him. He believes in you Peter, so I will get the boys ready for breakfast and afterwards, would you spend an hour with him?"

"Yes, Dad. I will help John and let him call his

grandparents, and we will call his Mom and Dad. I'm sure Jerry will be a big help today. John and Jerry have been good friends."

Peter did let John call his grandma, and called his parents also. He had trouble contacting them at first.

Peter and John went for a ride together and Peter said, "John where do your parents live?"

"They live far away," said John. "They travel a lot, and when they are home they don't want me around. They think I am too much trouble. That's why I was going by my grandmother's. Mr. Watkins, I would like to talk to them."

"Would that be okay with you, John?"

"You mean they would come to the school and I would get to see them? Yeah, that would be okay, but...but what if they don't come? Then what?" asked John with tears running down his cheeks.

"John," said Peter, "if they cannot come to the school I will take you to see them. I think I can help you and your Mom and Dad become a family. Will you trust me and want me to help?"

"Yes sir!" said John and wiped the tears away.

"Okay, now how about a hamburger and ice cream?" asked Peter.

John was all excited, "Yeah!" No one had ever treated him like this. It made him feel good and he knew Peter was his friend and cared about him.

Peter and John finished talking over a hamburger and fries, and then returned to join the other boys.

"John, I must go get rest now. So will you promise me to let us know if you want to talk? Mr. Watkins is a very good listener too. That's how I got my faith and my real Mom and Dad, just let him know if you need to talk okay?"

"Oh okay, Peter, I will. Thank you for taking me for a ride."

Peter gave John a hug and let George know he was going home. "See you at home Peter, and thank you for staying later. Bye now."

Peter continued working at the boy's school for his Dad through the summer. He had accomplished what he set out to do. He was at the school for two years and had saved enough to pay for his tuition at college. He was proud of Jerry and John. They had come a long way to becoming good boys and best friends. He was proud of all the boys. They had learned what and who God was. John and Jerry's parents came to visit more often and learned about God and became close families of God.

Then the summer ended for Peter, but the boys school wouldn't let him go without giving him an appreciation party for all his help and asked if he would be back. "I will be back, you can count on it," said Peter.

The boys and staff sang a farewell song and John presented Peter with a gift from all the boys and the parents and staff.

"We will all miss you, Peter. We have learned a lot from you being here."

Peter was proud to accept the gift, but was sad to have to say goodbye and would never forget them all.

"Thank you very much, each and every one of you. I will miss you all, but I will be back. I know my father Geroge will keep you all safe and you can talk to him anytime. Remember that, okay? Well, God bless you all and thanks again. I am proud and thank God I could give back a little of what the Watkins' have given me - a home, love, and understanding that I needed." And they joined in with the farewell party.

College in Minneapolis

Peter continued to help the boys. His Dad and Mom were proud of the way the boys had grown love for one another and became good men who could help others. Jerry and John began going to bible classes and visiting their parents on weekends. Many of the boys came to the school as Jerry and John did, but found that life isn't all that bad.

Summer was over and Peter had to prepare for college where he could become the best minister he could be and teach the word of God to others who were lost. It would be the first time he was going to be alone without his mother and father there to talk to. It would be lonesome he thought. One evening before he was to leave,

George and Lynda sat by the fireplace. They were going to miss Peter.

Peter came downstairs from packing, and Lynda said, "Peter, would you join us for a while?"

"Sure Mom , I would love to. I guess we all feel something is going to be missing in us."

"Yes son, it will be lonely without you here at night. But we will know you are studying hard and will call every week."

Geroge said, "college will keep you busy, but if you need anything you just call, okay?"

"I will," said Peter, "but I will be fine - except I know it will be lonesome at first."

Peter was going to college in Minneapolis, a very good college. He knew he would like it. Days passed and it was the day Peter left for the airport. George and Lynda drove him so they could see him off. They hugged, and Peter kissed his Mom and said "Goodbye and take care" to both of them. As George and Lynda watched as the plane was going out of sight, they began to shed a few tears and walked to the car.

They stopped at the boy's school to see how things were. It seemed empty at first because Peter wasn't going to be there, but then John and Jerry came over to them and talked, they were glad to see them. They visited for a while before they went out to eat and then home. How different it seemed to them to go home that night.

"Well Lynda," said George, "we are alone, but we can always call Peter and he will be here on vacations. So we have that to look forward to don't we?"

"Oh sure, George."

"He will be home before we know it, the time will go by fast. He has a long time to go for the teachings of God. It will be at least 4 years, but he will be home again. So, let's thank God for giving us Peter and maybe someday he will get married and we will have little grandchildren."

"Oh yes George, I would love that," Lynda replied, "a little one around here again."

As they sat by the fireplace reading, they couldn't help but wonder if Peter had gotten there yet. It was quiet and they were ready to go to bed, when the phone rang.

"Hello?" said Lynda.

"Hi Mom ," Peter answered. "I wanted to call you and Dad and let you know I made it okay."

"Good Peter," said Lynda. "I am so glad you called. I will let you talk with your Dad. We love you son."

As she handed the phone to George. "Hi son," he said, "are you okay?"

"Sure Dad, I miss you and Mom , but I am fine. The plane ride was good. I met another student that was going to the same college. So I will be fine Dad."

"I am glad you called son. I guess you're tired from the ride. So I will let you go and will call you tomorrow. We love you."

"I love you both," said Peter, and they said their goodbyes. Lynda felt good that Peter had called, and could now rest easy.

It was hard getting to sleep that night for Peter and his parents. Peter had a room overlooking the lake, he loved that. He liked seeing the seagulls fly around with their wings spread out wide. They were beautiful. He wondered how God could calm the sea and make things so beautiful. After seeing that he could go to sleep knowing his Mom and Dad were okay, and the boys at school would have to get to know and trust another person, but Dad would be there.

Monday arrived and Peter had to find his room for class. He had many classes and houses to study, if he was going to do what God had planned for him - and he wanted to make his parents proud, because they had given him so much all these years. So he was going to make them happy the way they did for him.

The first few months were hard and there were students who were there because their parents wanted them to. That was not easy for them as Peter could tell. Working at the boys school, he could tell what students had problems at home and those who didn't. Sometimes he would call home and discuss it with his Dad and that would help, but they were grown people, should he enter fear, or just let them come to him? Peter was glad if one of them asked him questions. Some of them didn't always like the answer Peter gave them.

Peter kept to himself a lot, unless there was someone who wanted to talk to him. He was always willing to listen. After Peter was settled in college, and met several students who were in the same courses, he had planned to go home for Christmas vacation. He wouldn't miss that to see his mother's and Dad's surprise look for anything.

They heard a knock on the door, but they weren't expecting Peter. As George opened the door, Lynda heard him say, "Peter! Oh we are so happy to see you!" Lynda said, "why didn't you tell us?"

"I wanted to surprise you for Christmas," said Peter. "Merry Christmas Mom and Dad."

"Merry Christmas," they said. "Well, come in, you must be cold. Come on by the fireplace and warm up."

They had a good visit and didn't want to think of Peter going back, but they knew it had to be. The week went by fast and Peter returned to school. He wasn't interested in girls, but would talk with them until the second year of college. He had met a very pretty girl in his class. She didn't give Peter the time of day, because she knew she couldn't get involved if she was going to pass her grades. She was having trouble with them. It was something she wanted so much, she couldn't ask her Mom because she wasn't well, so she had no one to count on except herself. Peter noticed her, and after class went over by her.

"Hello, I'm Peter Watkins. I hope you don't think I am being too forward, but I couldn't help noticing how sad you are."

"Hi, I am Cindy. I am trying to study for an exam. If I don't pass, I have to drop out of school."

"Why?" asked Peter, "can't you take it over?"

"No. This is my second time. I guess I worry about my Mom too much," said Cindy.

"Well, would you like some help?" asked Peter.

Cindy Harper looked up at Peter, "How can you help me?" she said. "Besides, why do you care? I don't even know you."

Peter said, "It's true. We don't know each other, but I do care about people, and if I can help I would be glad to stay and help you. That is, if you would like."

"Well…okay…but…but…I can only stay one hour because my Mom is sick and she is home alone." Cindy was glad to get the help, but should she really accept it?

"I am sorry to hear that," Peter said. "I know what you are going through."

"How would you know Peter?" she asked. "You have no idea."

"Because I lost my Mom when I was very young. Mom was very sick. I was only twelve and stayed with her until God called her to join my father in Heaven."

"I am so sorry Peter. I didn't know. Would you like to see what I have to do?" said Cindy.

Cindy and Peter studied for her exam and then

walked to their dorm. Their dorms were across the road from each other. The two of them were quiet and Cindy said, "Thank you Peter. Wish me luck, okay!"

"I will pray for you," he said. They said, "goodbye, see you tomorrow in class," and left with a smile.

They did see each other in class and began seeing each other often. They were getting serious about their relationship and it was good. Peter had met Cindy's Mom several times and prayed that Cindy wouldn't lose her like he did his parents.

Now it was time for George and Lynda to meet Cindy. First he would write and ask if it was okay to bring her. Cindy was also studying discipleship.

George and Lynda were glad Peter was finally going to bring his girl home to meet them. Her mother was well again and she could leave for a weekend.

When Peter arrived with Cindy at his home, George and Lynda greeted them with open arms. "Hi Peter! How are you son?" His Mom asked, and George hugged him and shook his hand.

"So, this is the young lass we have heard so much about? Welcome to our house, come on in."

Peter said, "Cindy this is my mother, Lynda, and my Dad, George Watkins."

Cindy felt comfortable with them and joined in on the conversation. It seemed like she had a lot in common with Peter and his family.

Then Peter's mother asked him a question that Peter couldn't answer. "Peter do you and Cindy have any plans for marriage?"

"Not yet, Mom , but when we do, you and Dad will be the first to know, We want to finish our college first, so it doesn't interfere with families and studies."

"Peter said you are also studying discipleship?" said Lynda. "Is that right?"

"Yes! I hope I can make it. It is a lot more work than I expected. I don't know what I would have done without Peter's help."

"I am glad he could help you," Lynda replied.

They talked all hours of the night. Peter's parents were getting tired and showed Cindy the guest room. Peter said good night and they went upstairs to bed.

In the morning, George and Lynda asked Cindy and Peter if they were going to church with them. "We would be proud to have you there with us."

Cindy answered, "we would love to go, wouldn't we Peter?"

"Oh yes," he said. "We always go together when we are home. My parents brought me up in this church. It's a beautiful church."

George was happy to hear Peter say that because he knew Peter meant so much to them. After church, they took Cindy to the boys school where Peter had seen John and Jerry. They were almost ready to graduate. "What young men they turned out to be," Peter thought.

"Well, Peter," Cindy said, "we better get ready to leave for the school. But first, let's take your folks out for lunch, okay?"

"We would love that," George said, "but lunch is on us this time, okay?"

They enjoyed their visit with the Watkins' and promised they would be back soon, as they said their goodbyes and were on their way back to college.

"What a lovely couple," Cindy said to Peter as they were driving.

"I think so too," Peter replied. "If it wasn't for them, I don't know what would have happened to me."

"You are very lucky Peter, and my mother and

I are lucky to have you as a good friend."

It was quiet for the rest of the way until they almost got to Cindy's home, and then Peter got to thinking, "Cindy, when we finish our college and get our degree in ministry, well, um will you marry me?" He wasn't sure of Cindy's reaction to his question.

As they looked at each other they smiled and Cindy's face was aglow. "Oh, yes Peter!" she said. "My mother will be so happy! She thinks you are wonderful."

Peter put his arms around her and said, "I love you Cindy."

"I love you too Peter," she said. "What about mother?" Cindy asked.

"We will take care of that when the time comes. Okay?" answered Peter.

Peter Graduates From College

Peter and Cindy went back to school with the last year being the hardest of all. They worked hard at their studies together. When the final week came and they were to graduate, they were very nervous and yet excited.

Peter and Cindy's parents were too proud of their children. After it was all over, Peter's Dad and Mom said, "What are you two going to do now Peter?" They were hoping they would move home.

"I'm not sure yet, Dad. Cindy and I thought we would see if you need someone at the school until we get a church who needs us, right Cindy?"

"Yes Mr. and Mrs. Watkins, I would like my

mother to move here also, so she will be close to us and we can watch over her."

Lynda said, "That would be good."

And George said, "there will always be a place at the school for you Peter. The boys will be glad to see you, and you are welcome too Cindy. We can always use a smiling face and a helping hand."

They drove home in silence. Lynda and George were happy that Peter would finally be home again for good. Cindy had left to go home to her mother's, but wouldn't be gone for long.

As they drove along, George asked Peter if he and Cindy have any plans, on that he hesitated.

"You know what we mean, son?"

"Yes Dad, I know what you mean, but we want to wait to tell you together."

"Alright!" They said full of excitement as George and Lynda looked at each other.

When they arrived home after the long drive, they were very tired and had stopped for something to eat. Peter was very proud of his parents who had given this chance to become what his Mom and Dad Glennis wanted for him. They sat quietly by the fire and Peter thanked them.

"Mom and Dad, you are both wonderful. If it wasn't for you both, I couldn't have done it." said

Peter. "I love you both," and hugged them.

"Well, I better call Cindy and let her know we are home safely, and then I will call it a night. How does that sound Mom ?"

"That's a very good idea," said George.

Very tired looking George said, "You bet Lynda." As they went upstairs they said goodnight to Peter.

"Goodnight Mom and Dad," Peter said.

Peter called Cindy and talked for a long time, hesitating to hang up the phone, "Well," said Peter, "I better let you go and will see you this weekend. We will find a place where you and mother can be happy and comfortable."

The next two weeks were busy for all the Watkins' family. They had found a place that Cindy liked for her mother and her until that big day.

They had set the wedding day and everyone was very busy preparing for it. Lynda and George were so happy to see their son grow into a happy and responsible person. They said to each other, "we are very lucky parents, aren't we?" said Lynda.

"We certainly are dear," he said.

The Wedding

Peter and Cindy got her mother settled into a house near Peter's parents. Lynda and Cindy's Mom got along well and enjoyed each other's company. Mrs. Harter he wasn't too well, so being near neighbors was comforting to her.

"So when will the time will come and our children will be having their own family?" Mrs. Harter said.

"I cannot wait to see your first grandchild," said Lynda, "we were never able to have our own and when we found Peter it was a godsend. You have been our pride and joy for years, as you will feel about your children."

"You are a very special person to have found him - not many would take a boy in off the street and be able to adopt and have him love you so much. You are very lucky," Mrs. Harter said.

"I thank God for him. He came to us in a very discouraging time. George wanted to adopt and I wanted our own, but God made the choice for us and we love Peter very much," said Lynda.

After visiting with Mrs. Harter, Lynda said, "well I must be going home. George will be home from the boys school soon. You take care, and if you need us please feel free to call, and you are always welcome to come over anytime."

George and Peter returned home soon after Lynda did and were tired. They all sat down for the meal and Peter asked them if a fall wedding would be OK with them. "I think a fall wedding would be wonderful," said the Watkins', "it is such a beautiful time of year. Is that what you and Cindy agreed on?" replied Lynda.

"Yes mother, Cindy suggested it. She likes the fall colors of the trees, and the smell of fresh air."

"Well done Son," George said. "How about it? Did you pick a time and place?"

"Well yes, but I want to wait until Cindy comes, she should be over soon with her mother."

As they finished the evening meal and got the dishes out of the way, Cindy and Mrs. Harter had come and they were all excited about the wedding and all the plans to be made. It was so great to know their son was going to be married and someday give them grandchildren. But it wouldn't be so soon because they had to get a home and save for the one thing they wanted to do. They wanted to go on a honeymoon to the one place in their hearts, and it was the holy land in Jerusalem, where God's creations in history. Where they thought they could learn a little more about the Bible and how things happened in those days.

Peter and Cindy had a beautiful fall wedding. The colors were so magnificent - beautiful reds and browns and oranges. The bride wore a beautiful gown with a long train, she was a very pretty bride. Peter looked as handsome as anyone had seen him. There was a glow of happiness on his face until he remembered his Mom and Father Glennis and his face melted into a sad one.

George noticed it and asked Peter, "what's wrong? Are you having second thoughts?"

"Oh no, Dad. It's not that at all. I was just thinking of my real Mom and Dad and I know they are watching over us. I love you too, Dad. I hope you and -"

George interrupted Peter and said, "I understand

Peter. It's only natural you would feel this way, but they are smiling down at you and are very happy. Just as we are, we love you Peter."

Peter's smile came back, and he said, "thanks Dad, you're wonderful. God couldn't have given me a more caring and loving father. Someday Cindy and I want to give you and Mom a grandchild. I know it will make you both happy, and God will grant it for you and Mom .

"That will make your mother so very happy, Peter. Mom has always wanted a baby in the house, but God had other plans. Your mother expected it, and now to have a chance to be a grandparent - how wonderful it would be for her!"

They had a large wedding at the church with many friends from the boys school and some from college. They were so happy after the wedding day was over. George and Lynda took Mrs. Harter home. Peter and Cindy went off on their own, as a newlywed couple does. Well, Peter and his bride were only gone for a few days to be alone, and George missed them. They visited Cindy's mother often to make sure she was okay. Mrs. Harter was always glad to see them and she enjoyed their company.

The Watkins had something in mind and

asked Mrs. Harter if she would like to go for a ride with them.

"I would love to go," Mrs. Harter replied. "Can I bring anything?"

"Oh no, we just want to show you something and would like your opinion on it," said George.

"Okay," said Mrs. Harter, and she got in the car and enjoyed the ride and wondered what the surprise was. "Oh, and please call me Mary. Where are we going?"

"We are almost there, I think you'll like it when you see it. We thought it would be a great wedding gift for both of them, and we hope you do too. It was George's idea."

Mary was excited and couldn't wait to see what it was, when they pulled up to a beautiful little house with a picket fence around it.

"Is this the surprise?" Mary asked, her face full of smiles.

"Yes," George answered, "come on in and see what you think of it. We thought it would be a start for them, and a place they can raise their children - yours and our grandchildren."

As they walked up to the house they stopped and looked around, and then Mary said, "Well let's go in!"

She was so happy that her daughter and her son-in-law we're going to have a home to call their own - something she never had for her family.

"This is just the right size, and very nice for the young couple," said Mary. "They will love it!"

"We are very glad you agree, Mary, because we want you to always feel like part of the family. God has brought us together to be one of his families. God is the center of our lives. When he brought her to us, it was a miracle. And now we have a daughter to share with you. I hope we didn't make you feel it was just from Lynda and I, because it isn't. What do you think? George asked.

"It's from all of us. God has truly blessed these two young people with good parents."

"I think it's wonderful, and a nice little house to raise a family," Mary replied and she continued on to say, "and when we are gone to heaven, they will always have this house and home they can remember their family. Oh, I want to be a part of it, so what can I give to help out?" asked Mary. "I don't have a lot, but I would like to share in it."

"We thought you would Mary, so we made a list of things the house needed, and we want you to feel free to put anything in it that you feel you can afford. Is that alright with you Mary?"

"Oh yes," Mary said with a happy and excited expression on her face, with a few tears mixed in. "Thank you for understanding and being so thoughtful. God bless all of you."

As they walked through the house, they named things they could put in it and colors they thought that the couple would choose, but would leave it up to Peter and Cindy. When they left the house, driving and looking back at it, they knew it would be filled with happiness. George and Lynda took Mary home after they stopped to eat. She was very tired and had to lie down because she was just getting her strength back. She was an older person and hasn't been well for a while. The Watkins' promised Cindy they would look after her while they were gone.

"We will help you in Mary, and then we have to check on the boys at the home. But if you ever need us, just call okay?"

They got Mary settled and said goodbye. They stopped at the school to see how the boys were.

"Hi Mr. and Mrs. Watkins," they heard this voice that sounded very cheerful and turned to see John and Jerry helping with some of the younger boys.

George walked over to them and said, "Hi, how are you boys doing? It has been a while since I have seen you."

"We are fine Mr. Watkins. God has come into our lives and we try to help others. Has Peter come back?" asked Jerry.

"No, he is on his honeymoon remember? He got married, but he will be back Monday. I am very proud of you boys. How are your parents John?"

"Oh they are fine, they are coming this evening for a visit. We talk and get along very well."

"Well boys, we must go now. But anytime you want to stop and talk you just call okay?" George continued on to the office to check on things there, it was okay so they went home. Tired as they were, they went and sat by the fireplace for a little while and discussed how it would be quiet without Peter and how nice it would seem to have little children running around.

"That will come soon enough," George said, and then they retired for the night. It had been a long week for them. Peter and Cindy would return Sunday, and they wanted to have a welcome home party for them. So that Sunday in church they invited Mary and several of their friends over to welcome them home along with the minister and his family.

That night, Peter and Cindy had arrived home early. When there was no one around they went and looked around and found a note that George and Lynda had left on the table. It read: "Please meet us at this address - 915 S Ash St. It's about four blocks, we are meeting someone there. See you soon, love Mom and Dad."

Peter looked up the address over and then said, "well, let's put our things upstairs and then we will go okay?"

Meanwhile in the new house, George and Lynda were preparing a welcome home party, and many friends along with the pastor and his wife, were patiently waiting for Peter and his new bride. Then suddenly with lights out they heard a car pull up.

"It's them, everyone quiet please," said Mary Harter.

Her and the rest went into the kitchen and waited quietly.

"What are we doing here?" Cindy asked Peter. "I don't even know who owns this place."

"Well, let's go find out who does and see Mom and Dad."

They walked up to the door and stopped before going in, and said "this is a beautiful house. I wouldn't mind owning this myself," said Cindy.

"It is very nice," replied Peter. "Well I guess we better knock and see what's up."

So they knocked and a man opened the door and said, "are you Mr. and Mrs. Peter Watkins?"

"Yes!" Peter said. "Are my mother and father here? We were told to meet them here."

"Yes," said the man.

Peter had not recognized Mr. Wade, one of his Sunday school teachers. "Come on in, I will get them."

All of a sudden, everyone jumped out at once. "Surprise! Surprise!" Came from all directions, "Welcome home Peter and Cindy."

Surprised as they were they asked, "What is this for Mom and Dad?" Peter asked.

Cindy saw her Mom and gave her a big hug. "It is a welcome home party for the newlywed couple," said Mary.

"Come on in," said George. "You know most of the people from the church, and this is one of your Sunday school teachers Mr. Wade."

"Hi Mr. Wade. I'm sorry I didn't recognize

you. It has been a while," said Peter and then he introduced Cindy to him.

"Hello Mr. Wade, glad to meet you." t

The minister greeted both and said, "Congratulations we are glad you're back safe, and hope God never let you down. I know he won't."

They had their talks and ate so much they couldn't get over it, but made a toast to everyone and said, "thank you to everyone for the nice homecoming."

"Wait Peter! George has something he would like you and Cindy to have," said Lynda.

"What is it mother?"

He looked at Cindy and then at his Dad.

'Well son, your mother and Cindy's mother, and I went together and thought you would like to have this." He handed Peter the deed to the very house they're having their homecoming in.

Peter looked at it and asked, "What is it?"

He opened the envelope and looked at it with Cindy. They didn't know what to say.

"Wow," they both said. They were so surprised!

"I don't know what to say," Peter said.

They gave their parents a big hug and kiss. "Thank you so much, but you shouldn't have done it."

Cindy gave her mom a hug and they cried together.

Peter turned to everyone and said, "can we take each other's hand around the table? I would like to say prayer."

Peter praised God and all the friends that had been so kind to him and Cindy. "We thank you all for making this a happy homecoming. We are surely blessed with many friends and wonderful families. Amen."

Soon the crowd was saying goodbye to Peter and Cindy and wishing them well. Mr. and Mrs. Watkins stayed until it was over and helped clean up, along with Mrs. Harter. They were all tired but happy.

"Well," said Lynda, "you haven't looked or seen the whole house yet, we will show it to you and you can let us know how you like it."

As they toured the house, Mrs. Harter felt weak and Cindy took her mother to her room to lie down for a while.

"No Cindy, I would like to go home and rest if it is okay? I will be okay."

"Sure Mom, but we will stay with you for a while. Lynda and I will take you home."

Lynda and Cindy said, "we are going to take

Mary home, and will see that she is resting and be back soon okay?"

"Okay," said Peter and George, "We will pray for her and we will wait for you and Cindy."

Peter and George talked and were glad to have the time to themselves. Peter couldn't thank his Dad enough for all he had done.

"Son," said George, "your mother and I wanted to give you and Cindy something that would last forever. A place you can raise your children."

"We really love it Dad, and God knows we will always keep you and Mary in our hearts. I wonder how she is, maybe we should go see her Dad?"

"Sure son, we will go see."

They got in the car and drove over to find the doctor looking in on Mary, and Cindy sitting by her side with tears in her eyes. Peter walked in to comfort her.

"Darling, what is wrong? What did the doctor say?" This wasn't very easy for Peter, but he had to be strong for her and her mother.

"Peter, she had a heart attack and the doctor said she isn't going to make it. I don't want her to go yet," said Cindy.

"I know darling," said Peter. "I felt the same way when my real mother died. It was very hard, but

God calls us to a peaceful and beautiful world of His when it is time for us to go. Come on, let's pray for her."

As they prayed a peaceful feeling came over Mary's face and they knew that she was in heaven with the Father. The doctor asked them to leave the room, so they went out by Peter's Mom and Dad and embrace them and cried together.

As the days passed things got easier, but like Peter, Cindy would never forget her Mom. She would know that she would join her grandma and Dad in God's upper room, and that was a beautiful memory for her.

Peter went to work at the Christian boys home for his father, Cindy helped in the evening but went back to do some Bible study classes. Sunday was Peter's first chance at giving a sermon at the church. The pastor was going to be out of town and Reverend Marcus had asked Peter if he would like to give the sermon.

"Oh yes," said Peter.

Excited and yet scared, "what will I talk about?" Peter asked.

"You are a very good man, Peter. You'll find it in your heart."

"Okay Reverend," Peter said, "I will do my best.

Thank you for the faith you have in me. I won't let you down. Cindy will be by my side, won't you sweetheart?"

"Yes Peter, I sure will. I am proud of you," she said.

Peter and his parents greeted the congregation at the door with many smiling faces and Cindy next to him on Sunday morning. The sermon began with an introduction, which Peter hardly needed.

"Good morning," Peter said. "I am Peter Watkins. I am filling in for Reverend Marcus today and I hope I can get the word of God to you as well as your pastor does. Please," said Peter, "turn your song book to page 272."

The congregation sang "Just As I Am" loud and clear, giving Peter the sign that no matter who he was he was good and welcomed.

At the end, Peter asked the congregation to join him in the Lord's Prayer and the Benediction. When they shook hands with Peter they told him he did a good job and hoped he would come back soon.

"Peter," George said, "you did an excellent job. Your mother and I are proud of you."

"Thank you Dad, that means a lot to Cindy

and I. Oh Mom and Dad, why don't you come over and have dinner with us. Cindy and I would like that okay?"

"We would love to Peter," Lynda said, "we will see you in about an hour if that's all right?"

"That is fine Mom, see you later."

George and Lynda went to the boys' home, they wanted to surprise Peter with a couple of guests. They had asked Jerry to come with them. The boys loved it because they were going to see Peter. George asked the boys and their eyes lit up so bright and said "yes Mr. and Mrs. Watkins, we would love to see Peter's new house," answered Jerry all excited.

"Well now, Peter doesn't know that you were coming, so it is a surprise," the Watkins' said.

"Okay, we will be quiet," the boys said.

They left for Peter's and wondered if he would make them say grace. Peter did ask the boys to say grace with everyone, and they did well. The boys loved the house and had a chance to see Peter and his new wife. When the Watkins' took them back, the boys thanked them for a good time and for asking them to go.

"We had a good time, Mr. Watkins," replied the boys. And, "we will see you tomorrow," and said their goodbyes.

George and Lynda went home as happy as any parents could be.

"Well dear, we have a lovely family, a good home and boys that appreciate people now. I mean John and Jerry, they're leaving next year to go to school and live a good life. I am very proud of our school aren't you? It has been God's gift to us.

"Oh yes dear, very proud. Especially of the men who put God back into their lost lives and showed them the way home Lynda said.

George took Lynda's hand and said, "thank you dear. I couldn't have done it without you," and he kissed her on the cheek.

When they reached home, they looked at the wedding pictures of the kids and were so happy.

"I never thought we could be so happy," Lynda said. "God has given us everything a person could want."

"He really has dear, no one can ask for more. Well I guess I am going to read the Bible and then we can retire for the night. Does that sound good to you?" He asked.

"It sure does," Lynda said, and sat down beside him and listened.

Peter Accepts a Church

As Peter and Cindy start their new life in their new home, they wondered how did they become so rich from God's love with such great parents and two mothers who are in heaven. They were happy to be alone for a while.

They walked together through the house and Cindy said to Peter, "are you happy Peter, isn't this beautiful?"

"Oh yes, darling. We have so much to be happy about don't you think so?" He said. "God has really given us so much more than we deserve."

Peter said Cindy, "do you think that you would like children?"

"I thought we would have two. Your parents would like, that a boy and a girl. I thought it would be nice, but let's wait until our lives settle down okay?"

Cindy was finishing up her Bible classes, and Peter went back to the boys home as a Pastor in their little chapel where the boys go on Sunday. He loved talking to all of them.

One year later, he had gotten a phone call asking him if he could meet Reverend Marcus and the church committee at 2:00 p.m. at church Wednesday. He was anxious to tell Cindy about the phone call. Cindy and his parents met Peter at the house and asked Peter what was wrong.

"Nothing," he said, "Cindy and I want to share something with you."

"What is it Peter? Tell us."

"Okay, he said putting his arms around his wife."

"Is it what we think it is are you going…"

Peter interrupted his Mom, but knew what she meant. "No," said Cindy, "Peter can tell you okay?"

Peter got up and walked over by his Mom and Dad and then said, "Mom, Dad, I got a phone call the other day from Reverend Marcus. He wants me to meet him and the church committee on Wednesday. I don't know what it means, but I hope he has a church for us. Cindy and I are excited but cautious."

George got up and embraced Peter and

Cindy and him, "we're happy" even if it wasn't what they wanted to hear.

Wednesday came and the meeting was sad, and yet happy because Reverend Marcus was retiring, and happy because Peter was asked to be the new pastor to their church. Reverend Marcus said, "we will be proud to have you here Peter. The committee has agreed to it since I am going to retire soon, and that you and your wife would be an excellent candidate. You will have two months before you have the church, but we need your answer as soon as possible Peter."

Cindy and Peter looked at each other and said, "may we tell you now?"

"Sure," Reverend Marcus answered.

Peter was pleased with them for asking him, "How can we say no?" He said to them. "We would be proud to accept the offer. Thank you all!"

"Thank you, Peter!" said the committee group, "we have made a good choice."

"Wow!" Said Peter, "we are going to have our own church. We have certainly been blessed Reverend, but we will miss your preaching. You have been here since I was a young boy and the Watkins' brought me home. Cindy and I will try to do as well as you have," and shook hands with everyone and thanked them again.

He couldn't wait to stop and tell his Mom and Dad, which made them proud.

"Does this mean I won't see you at the boys school Peter?" Asked George.

"Oh no," said Peter. "I will be there as often as we can, won't we Cindy?"

"Of course we will, so Dad don't think you can get rid of us that easy," she said.

They had supper and talked about the pulpit and what they must do to prepare. The Watkins were proud of their son, and said, "See you tomorrow Son," and hugged Cindy.

Peter and Cindy arrived home a little while later than usual, but for a good cause.

"Well it is late dear," he said, taking her hand and sat by the fireplace as they read the Bible and prayed together for the offer that God had given them and said, "thank you Lord for choosing me and my wife for your work."

Weeks passed and Peter and his family were all preparing for church sermons. When the first Sunday came, they had welcomed Peter and his family, and said their goodbyes to Reverend

Marcus. The change was a time of accepting people and getting to know them and feeling comfortable. He knew the change would be a good one as he thought of his real Mom and Dad Glennis. They too would be happy for him, but he knew they were looking down upon him always, and that thought made him feel better.

They started their lives as happy as anyone could be because God had given them so much. Cindy and Peter joined his parents for breakfast the Sunday he was to give his first sermon. Peter was nervous and yet anxious to be a part of God's work. George said to Peter, "we better get to church so you have time to get your robe on, okay?"

"Yes Dad, we are ready to go aren't we Cindy?"

"Yes dear," she answered.

The sermon went well and greeting the people was a pleasure. Peter was content, and he decided to spend the rest of the day with Cindy together. It was a happy time for them. They settled into the ministry with pride and helped his Dad at times at the school. He was there he talk to John and Jerry. They were changed young men, and wanted to help other people. As they had graduated they had gone out to teach school and help other disturbed youth. Peter and the Watkins were proud of their school, and it would always be a part of their lives. But now, their son was moving on to new things. As the years passed, Peter and Cindy thought about having a family of their own. She became pregnant and she knew Peter's parents would love to hear they were going to be grandparents.

She told Peter the news Peter she said, "what dear?" She answered, as he looked up from his work.

"I have some news to tell you. I saw the doctor and we're going to have a baby," she waited for his response and wasn't sure of his feelings.

But Peter got up and gave her a big hug and said with a big smile on his face, "we are going to be parents! Mom and Dad are going to be grandma and grandpa!"

They have waited for this day. "Let's go tell them tomorrow."

"Okay," Cindy said as they just enjoy the news together.

Being a parent sounded great, but scary.

New Parents

Being new parents, Cindy and Peter couldn't wait to tell George and Lynda the news. It made them so proud. Lynda and George couldn't have children, but God granted them a son that they couldn't love anymore than if he was born to them. So when Peter went over after supper to give them the good news, Cindy said to Peter, "Peter let me tell your Mom and Dad may I?" Wishing her mother was here to hear.

"Sure Cindy," Peter said.

So Cindy began by taking a set of baby shoes out of her bag and held them out. "What do you think of this Mom and Dad? Aren't they pretty cute, they are so tiny."

Lynda smiled and took them in her hands. "Oh Cindy! Is it really true? Are you and Peter going to have a baby?" She hugged Cindy with happy tears.

"Yes Mom and Dad," Peter replied, "you're going to be grandma and grandpa. How does that sound?"

George shook Peter's hand and then congratulated the kids and said, "now we will finally have another child in our house, will you let us help you with them?"

"Of course you may! You have done more than you would like," said Peter.

"Oh no," George said and, "I want to love them as much as we do you, Peter."

"Thank you both," said Cindy, "we were hoping you would like having a little one around."

"Oh we will. We are going to retire soon and want to be able to spend time with you two and our grandchildren."

Months passed and since she was having a hard time carrying the baby, she had to stay off her feet so Lynda kept her in her house in bed. Peter would come home after work and stay with her. Being the first baby, it was all new to them and Lynda because she never had the privilege to give birth, but was glad to have Peter. As the time got close, Peter was home as much as he could because he knew God would help take care of them and give them a beautiful, healthy child. He didn't want to miss the chance of God giving him a chance to help bring a child into the world.

One month later it was time for delivery day. Cindy was resting and Lynda thought she heard her call, so she went in and Cindy said, "call Peter, Mom, please. I think it's time," and she started to groan as labor had started.

"Okay dear, right away, just relax."

She called George and had him and Peter come home. She had called the doctor, and he came as soon as he heard, then George and Peter were there. They were walking the floor waiting patiently for the doctor to come in and tell them. When he did come out he had a look on his face and none of the family could make out.

"Well! What's wrong is she Okay? Doctor,. tell us" said Peter.

George and Lynda couldn't wait to hear either, "tell us, doctor please."

The doctor wiped his hands and shook hands with Peter and his parents. "Brace yourselves," he said, "it is a set of twins, a boy and a girl."

"Twins?" Asked Peter, "we didn't expect that.

Oh man, what are we going to do? We only have one crib."

"Don't worry Peter, we will help Cindy while you're at work. It will be fine," they both said. "After all we are the grandparents, and don't they always spoil the grandchildren?"

"Why don't you and Cindy stay for a couple of days until you get used to them? They are going to need a lot of care, especially with two of them."

Peter and Cindy loved the twins and called them Hope and George. They couldn't have been more proud than they were then. The grandpa and grandma Watkins loved caring and doing things with the children.

A Prayer for George

A year had passed, and the twins were walking and playing with each other, it was so cute to watch. George and Lynda enjoyed them very much until one day in spring, George took sick and Peter was at church. He called home and his mother answered with a sad voice and told Peter, "Peter your father has pneumonia, we need to take him to the hospital."

"We will meet you there after the service, Mom. He's going to be okay. God will take care of him. I will pray for him and be there soon."

He finished his sermon asking the congregation to pray with him for his father. They did and Peter said, "Amen," and left for the hospital.

When he got there, his mother and Cindy were waiting for him.

"How is he?" Peter asked. "Is he going to be okay?" looking down at his father.

"We don't know, son he's pretty sick, he wants to see you Peter," said Cindy, "he's been asking for you."

So Peter went in to see his father. "Hi Dad," Peter said, "I'm here, okay?"

"Peter, take care of your Mom for me will you?" George said in a little voice.

"Dad you can do it when you get well, but I will until you get home okay? Please Dad, don't leave us, we need you. Your grandchildren will miss you."

George drifted off to sleep and the nurse checked on him, "he is just sleeping," she said, "why don't you and your family use the chapel while he is sleeping, we will call you when he awakes."

"Okay," they said and went to say a prayer for George. "Please God," said Peter, "don't take him yet, he is needed here on earth we need him," they shed tears together.

Cindy turned to Peter and his mother and said, "should we go back to see Dad?"

They returned to George's room and saw he was resting. Peter picked up the Bible and read out loud as he always had when he was a little boy. He read the 23rd psalm. Peter heard a voice, and felt George take his hand.

Peter answered, "I'm here Dad how are you? We are all okay, the children are fine."

"I love you," George said. Lynda stayed and she sat by his side all night while Peter and Cindy went home to the twins.

Hope was crying and Cindy picked her up and calmed her down. "You are a sweetheart, mommy loves you, now take your bottle and go to sleep."

Then Cindy started singing lullabies to her as Hope fell asleep. George had already been to sleep as Peter looked in on him. "Well," said Peter, "this has been a long day for you dear, so let's get some rest while the twins are sleeping."

"I agree darling," replied Cindy.

Morning broke early with the sun shining through their windows. As they awoke, they dressed and fed the twins and took them to the day care center, and they were to see George in the hospital before going to the church. George had been a little better and they had sat him up to eat.

"Dad it is good to see you sitting up. How are you?" asked Cindy.

"I'm tired, but a little hungry. Will you take Lynda home Cindy? Please she needs to get her rest."

"I will be glad to," Cindy answered, "we will come back later to see you."

Lynda gave her husband a kiss and said, "See you later dear, goodbye."

George recovered and was able to go home to see the twins. He couldn't wait to hold them and tell them stories. Growing up with the Glennis's was great, Peter knew what it was to have nothing but love and now he had the love of God, and the promises that his real Mom told of God. She wanted Christian people to take care of him, and parents that gave him a home, a family of his own, and now a church chosen for him. He couldn't have been more blessed than he already was, and will always thank God for that, and his Dad, George Watkins, who found him.

Part 2

Blessed

Being blessed by Christian parents, Peter wanted his children to have the same upbringing that he had. People who are homeless and lost and needed special care like he did; he wanted to give his twins a good Christian life.

Hope, their little girl, was beautiful. She had dark hair and brown eyes as Peter's mother had and she was going to be a picture of her mother. George, while he had his own little features and funny little smile, he was full of energy and kept Cindy busy every minute except when they were at daycare.

Lynda and George were so happy to be called grandparents, and are the proudest people there could be on earth. They accomplished so much for themselves, and wanted the same for Peter and his family.

They had been blessed with a life that God wanted for them. And now recovering from his illness, George Sr. wants to spend time watching their grandchildren grow into good, young Christians as they have done for Peter.

Cindy and Peter continue to minister at their church and the congregation was growing, he was proud to be a part of it. Hope and little George were ready to start their first year of school.

"I can't believe it," said Cindy, "where did the time go? Our little twins are growing up right under our nose."

Hope and George were ready for kindergarten at 5 years old, and had to go see their doctor for shots and a physical before they entered school. After returning home, Cindy look concerned when she came home with the twins, especially Hope. Her darling little girl, how could anything be wrong? She looks healthy, why would the doctor tell her that Hope may have to come back? George seems to be fine, always full of energy and spirit, nothing could keep him down. That was good, even though she had her hands full with him, but she loves him very much as she does Hope.

Peter was home waiting for them when Cindy came in he said, "darling how did the exams come out? What did the doctor say?"

"Fine," Cindy replied. "Peter," she said "I need you to help me in the kitchen. The children are hungry, can you come please?"

"I will be right there," he said.

Peter put them in their chairs, gave them both a big hug and a kiss, and said "I love you little rascals come on let's have some lunch while mommy rests."

While Peter waited until they were done, the twins then went outside to play and little George saw a car pull up and called out "Grandpa!" and ran to them.

"Hi Grandpa!" said George as he picked them up in his arms.

"Gee you two are getting heavy for Grandpa."

They walked in the house to see Cindy and Peter. Cindy was up and saw them coming, while Peter was studying for his sermon on Sunday.

"Hi Cindy," they said, "your twins are getting big and beautiful."

"Yes they are," she said. "They start school in a few weeks. I think the teachers will have their jobs cut out for them."

"How did the children do on their physicals?" George asked.

"Well, George was fine. He got his shots and doctor said he's very healthy."

Peter waited for a few moments then looked at Cindy. "But what about Hope?" He asked, "how did her test come out? Was there something wrong, is she okay?"

The twins had gone back outside to play. Cindy wasn't sure how to answer Peter and his parents. "I don't know, I haven't heard from the doctor yet he will call us once he knows."

"What?" Peter asked.

"They will let us know what the blood tests are," she replied.

"She said they have to check in again for what?" asked Peter's Mom. "Is something wrong?"

"I don't know yet," said Cindy frustrated, "we can only pray that everything is okay for Hope's sake. The doctor mentioned something about protein deficiency - it will affect the kidneys if it's not treated."

"Well, Hope seems to be alert and eats good. He must be wrong."

Lynda replied, "let's hope so. She looks perfectly fine to us. Doesn't she George?"

"Yes, she sure does. She looks like a picture of health. Peter did you get any new members lately?" asked George.

"No Dad. Why do you ask?"

"Well, there's a new couple that moved in next door with two children. I thought they might have contacted you.

Peter didn't know the answer. "But they are welcome to come and visit our church. Have you met them yet?"

"No I thought your Mom and I will go see them and welcome them to our neighborhood."

His Mom and Dad visited for a while and Peter asked them to stay for supper. After supper they played with the twins and had fun with them, and it was time to put them to bed. They helped tuck them in and George gave his grandson a hug and a kiss goodnight.

George giggled and told his grandpa goodnight.

He walked over by Hope and wondered how she could have anything wrong. She is such a pretty girl, and he said to Cindy, "I can't imagine anything can be wrong," he tucked Hope in and gave her a hug and kissed her and said "goodnight my little angel, goodnight."

"Grandpa and Grandma," the twins said, "We love you."

George and Lynda told Peter and Cindy goodbye and they would see them later. "Let us know what you find out about Hope, okay? We love you." And they left for home but stopped at the Christian school first.

Peter and Cindy looked in on the twins as they were both sleeping sound and looked like little angels. "What are we going to do about Hope, our little girl?" Cindy asked.

We will take one day at a time, and let God help us through. He will watch over Hope for us okay? Let's go to bed and read our Bible and put it all in his hands. He will take care of it!" said Peter

They curled up together, Peter holding Cindy in his arms.

A few days later, the doctor called them and asked if they could meet at his office. Peter said yes and asked him if there was anything wrong.

"We will talk about it when you come in. See you soon," he said.

Peter holding Cindy in his arms said, "don't worry, I don't think it's going to be that serious honey. If it is, we will take care of it okay?" he comforted her and she felt that with Peter she could handle anything.

"Peter would you feel okay if I ask your mother and Dad to go with us?"

"Sure," he said, "anything you want dear. I think they would be glad you asked them. They love these kids, you know."

"Yes I know they do. Sometimes I wish my Mom was here."

And he said, "yes dear, I know how you feel."

"Peter I'm sorry. Your parents have been great, and I would love to have them come with us."

"It's okay darling."

Cindy called Peter's folks and asked if they would go with her and Peter to the doctors with them and they were happy to do it. The next morning, the sun came up bright and early, peeking through the curtains waking the little ones.

"Mommy! Daddy!" they called.

Peter and Cindy said, "what's wrong?" and they jumped on the bed with them and they enjoyed that time of morning with the two little ones.

"Well, we have to get up and get you ready for your daycare okay?" They tickled them and hugged them both and gave Cindy a good morning kiss

They got the children off to school and then went to the doctor's office. Peter's parents came to the house and followed them to the doctor's office. When they got out of the car, George asked, "Peter what's the doctor's name?"

"It's Dr. David Johnson," Cindy replied. "I heard it was a very good children's doctor, he was very nice to the twins."

Peter was thinking of his Mother Glennis, and wishing that Doctor Baker were still practicing. He was a doctor that took care of his mother, he would know what to tell Peter.

When they got to the clinic, Cindy introduced the family to a doctor and asked if they could sit in on the meeting.

"They certainly may," he replied. "It may be helpful to you and Peter," he said. "Come in," the doctor said, "I guess you are all a little curious."

Yes we are," George said. "My son and Cindy are very worried. Hope looks very healthy and alert how could anything be wrong?"

"Well, doctor," said Peter, "what do you think is wrong with our daughter?"

"First let me explain the x-rays and see if

you folks see anything different. If you don't understand, I will explain," replied the doctor.

The family did not see anything different. "We're sorry doctor, you'll have to show us," they said.

They all sat quietly while the doctor talked to them about the x-rays. "Hope has what we call PTC," the doctor said.

"What is that?" asked Cindy.

"It's a situation where she has too much protein, and it can affect the kidneys. It can be treated, but we are not sure if there's a cure for it or not," the doctor replied. "I don't want to alarm you, but if it isn't treated right away it may cause kidney failure. Hope is one of the lucky ones. We caught it in time."

"What can we do Dr. Johnson?" asked the family.

Dr. Johnson looked at the family and noticed they were worried. "Well," he said. "We need to get Hope started on a special diet."

"What type of diet?" asked Cindy.

"We put them on a protein free diet, which includes no milk, meat, or eggs or anything else that has protein in it. It will be very hard for her and for the parents at first," the doctor said.

"We will do anything you say Dr. Johnson," Peter replied.

"First we need to get Hope in the hospital to take tests, and then we will know where to start, okay?" said the doctor. "So I would like you to make an appointment to take her to the hospital so we can get started, It is very important to get started as soon as possible."

"How long will Hope have to stay in the hospital?" asked Lynda and George, looking at Cindy and Peter, they saw how upset the were.

"I'm not sure," said the doctor, "it would just be a little while until we can get the protein count worked out and balanced out. But remember," he said, "you will have to stick tight to her diet when she comes home from the hospital. It is very important to her health. There have been cases where the child has been cured only by the grace and prayers of God."

Peter and Cindy embraced each other and shed tears, but agreed of God was going to heal Hope. They would do everything necessary.

"Thank you very much, Doctor," Peter replied. "We appreciate your help."

"How do we explain this to our little girl? How is she going to understand what's going on, and what will she do when she can't eat all the things she has been eating?"

So many questions to be able to answer for Hope, but how do we tell her these were questions that Peter and Cindy asked themselves?

"Ho can we help our little girl, mom?" said Peter, "this is going to be bigger than we can handle."

"Now you listen here," Lynda said to both of them. "Who helped you through your troubles when your parents died? And who was the one that led you to our home Peter?"

"I'm sorry Mom, Dad." Peter said. "I know God brought me to you, I'm just worried. I know I have to put our trust and faith in God. If it wasn't for you and Dad and God I probably wouldn't be here today. So Cindy and I will keep our prayers going for her and keep her safe like you both did for me. I love you Dad and Mom," said Peter and he gave them a hug thank you.

They prepared Hope for her visit to the hospital, and told her she had to go so she could get well.

"I'm not sick Daddy," said Hope.

"Come here my little angel," said Cindy. "When we go to the hospital, you will see other little children also, and the doctor will be there okay? So don't be scared. Daddy and I will be right by your side."

The time had come. Peter and Cindy met the doctor at the hospital. "We tried to tell her Doctor Johnson, but she doesn't understand."

"Peter," said the doctor, "may I talk to you and Cindy?"

"Of course," he said.

"Okay," the doctor said, "let me talk to Hope alone. Maybe I can help her to understand that it will help her get better and to get ready for what she has to do."

"Okay," Cindy and Peter agreed with a doctor along with George and Lynda. When they finished with the doctor, and Hope had become more relaxed, they arranged Hope to stay at the hospital. Hope was placed in a room with another little girl who's going through the same thing. The nurse talked to Hope, and Hope liked her because she was very nice and could make children laugh and smile.

When hope was settled in her room, her Mom and Dad told her they were going to get something to eat. "No Mom, don't leave me. Please, I don't want to stay Daddy, I want to go with you and Mommy."

Hope was frightened. "Okay darling, we will stay," said Cindy. "Come here, sit on my lap. We won't leave you, but you must calm down."

"Where are Grandma and Grandpa?" Hope asked. "I want to see them. Can Grandma read me a story?"

" You will have to ask her."

"Okay," says Cindy.

"I will call them and Daddy will be here with you until they come, okay?"

Peter picked Hope up and walked a little way with Cindy. Cindy gave them both a hug and kiss. "I will be back and bring you something to eat, and maybe grandpa and grandma will come so you be a good girl. I love you." Cindy said as she left with tears in her eyes.

And looking back, Cindy called George and Lynda and told them Hope wanted them to come to the hospital. Cindy stopped and picked up something for their supper, and some hot coffee. She stopped at the chapel and prayed that God would give them all strength and courage to get Hope through this awful thing that had taken hold of their little girl's life.

"Why hope?" she asked God.

When she finished, she saw someone standing in front and he said to her, "everything is going to be alright. God will protect her from whatever is wrong."

Cindy felt God's hand on hers or an angel and she knew she would be there all the way for Hope. After that, she returned to the room where Hope was sitting in Grandpa's lap listening to a story and ready to fall asleep. Peter said, "Cindy you eat, and then you and your parents better get some rest. I will say tonight in case she wakes and is scared."

"Okay dear, but if you need me please call anytime."

Peter and his parents left after laying Hope in her bed. "I need to write my sermon yet for tomorrow, and we'll ask for prayers of healing for Hope," Peter told his parents and he said goodnight to them see you tomorrow.

George said, "Get a good night's sleep."

Peter was home alone to think and wonder how his little girl could be afflicted with this awful illness. "What is this, a test from God?" he thought as he fixed a cup of hot chocolate. He went to his office to plan his sermon for church. He prayed and asked God to give him the words and courage he needed to get through it, and as he finished his speech he grew very tired and decided to call it a day and fell asleep as soon as he hit the pillow.

Sunday morning came with the sun peeking through the windows and brought new hope. Peter called the hospital to see how Hope was, and told Cindy he and Grandpa would be there to say with Hope after church so she could come home and get some rest. Grandma would take care of little George.

Little George didn't understand where his sister was, so when he went to church with his Dad and Grandpa and Grandma, he asked, "Daddy where is Hope? Can't I see her please Daddy?"

"Yes Georgie, we will go see Hope after church," said Peter. "But after that, Grandma's going to take you home with her. Would you like that?"

"Oh ya!"

Little George loves playing with his grandparents. "I love my Grandpa and Grandma," said Georgie. "But I'll miss my sister. We have fun together."

"Well, your sister is going to be fine, and then you will be able to play with her again." Peter told George.

Hope was in the hospital for a week, and the doctor held her on his lap and explained to her how important it was that she did everything her parents wanted her to do, so God could help her get well. Hope listened to the doctor and said, "I will do what Mommy and Daddy tell me, and does Georgie have to do it too?"

"No sweetie," the doctor told her.

"He doesn't have this problem that you do. But I'm sure he will help you too. So little one, we are letting you go home okay?" and he hugged her and talked to the family about her diet and what they could expect.

It was very hard for the family at first. Cindy had watched them in the hospital and wondered how Hope would accept it. She put up a fuss at first and wouldn't eat. Cindy and Lynda talked to the nurse, but the nurse couldn't get her to eat either. So they called the doctor before they let Hope go home. The doctor came in and checked Hope's report and said to her, "I hear you're not eating."

He picked her up and sat her on his lap while Hope rubbed her eyes with tears in them and said, "because I don't like it."

"Well maybe we can find a different diet, but

you know you have to eat if you're going to get well. So will you try and promise?"

"Yes," said Hope.

"That's a good girl," said the Doctor as he gave her a hug, and he said, "stay with Hope until she starts eating."

"Very good," he told Hope. "That will make our little angel get stronger. When you go home you will help Mom and Dad by eating the things that are on your diet okay?"

Hope gave the doctor a hug and said, "Okay, I promise Doctor. And I will help Mommy."

As the doctor left, he told Peter if there was anything they needed to discuss, don't hesitate to call.

"Thank you, Doctor. We will."

"Hope can go home this afternoon," the doctor told Peter.

But before he left, he told her goodbye and that he had to go see another little girl.

"What's her name?" asked Hope.

"Well her name is Jenny. She wasn't as lucky as you."

"Why?" asked Hope.

"Because we didn't catch it early enough like we did yours," Dr. Johnson replied. "So you get a lot of rest and we will see you in 4 weeks, all right?"

"Bye, Doctor," Hope said with a smile.

Hope was released from the hospital. She had adjusted to a diet and schedule, and was anxious to go home to see her brother George and her other friends.

When Hope came home that day, she had a big welcome home party. A couple of her little friends came over and of course Grandma and Grandpa welcomed her with a hug. Georgie had lots of questions.

"How come you were in the hospital, Hope? he asked. "Are you okay?"

"I'm going to be fine," Hope replied. "The Doctor said I can't have meat or milk or cheese. I will be on a special diet, so I have to listen to Mommy and Daddy and the Doctor so I can get well."

Hope was pretty smart for her age. It was a week later when Cindy finally got the diet balanced out, making a special mild formula was a touchy thing her and Peter to learn together, so if one wasn't able to do it the other could.

Scheduling Hope's eating took a little remembering, because she had to eat more often and less.

"Hope, we'll need to schedule a visit for a check-up."

Peter told Cindy, "I will do that tomorrow, dear."

Cindy replied, "thank you for remembering."

Hope had a little bunny that she loved. Peter had brought it in to Hope. "I want to hold her, Daddy please. I love my bunny," she said.

Hope adjusted with her milk and her diet and was ready to start school with little George.

Peter and Cindy had taken them on their first day of school and explained Hope's situation to the teachers and asked that they help Hope remember to take her milk and a little something to eat at a certain time. "We are happy to do it." Mrs. Macey said - she is Hope and Georgie's kindergarten teacher.

Peter and Cindy had to go to the church while the kids were in school. Nowadays, they have kindergarten all day so that gives Mom and Dad's time to get things done and have time for the twins at night.

"What are you doing today?" Peter asked Cindy.

"I will help you at the office for a while, and then stop to see Dad at the School for Boys to see if there is something he needs," she replied, "and then home to the children. They have been so good to us and watching little George. I thought I would see if they needed help."

"That's very nice of you darling."

"Oh, I will pick the twins up from school, okay? So I will see you around 3." He hugged her and said, "I love you."

As the months passed, Hope was a happy little girl and enjoyed school. The other children were curious why she couldn't eat the things they could, but didn't ask questions just treated it as normal. Each year Hope was able to eat a little more, and drink her milk when she wanted to. Little George was very active. He loved soccer and swimming. He was like a little frog in water. He enjoyed sports of all kinds. Peter made sure that he save time to spend with the twins. It was a special time for them all to spend time together. Peter remember the time Mom and Dad Glennis spent with him when he was little, and wanted his twins to have the same. They would tumble in the grass, or play hide-and-go-seek, and enjoyed it all. George and Lynda stopped to visit Peter and the family every weekend to help with the twins.

George asked Peter if he would have time to see one of the boys at school.

"Of course, Dad. You know anytime you need me I will be there as you were for me. What is it you need help with, Dad?

"We just got a couple of boys in this week and I can't get them to join the other boys, and I thought you could see him as you did for John and Jerry. They turned out to be such good boys, and help me whenever they are home."

"I would be glad to see if I can help them Dad. But it might take a few days before they accept help from me."

"Thank you, Son," George said. "I know you can do it. You are a God sent for our School. The boys look up to you whenever you are there."

"Thanks, Dad. I will talk to them tomorrow around 2 if that's okay? I'll meet you at school."

George and Lynda had supper with the family. They enjoyed the grandchildren so very much.

"Grandpa, can I come home with you?" asked Hope.

He was really surprised and happy she wanted to go with them, it was the first time after coming home.

"Oh sweetheart, you have to go to school in the morning. But you know what? What if you and little brother come next weekend and stay with your grandma and I? Is that alright?"

"Can we Mom, Dad?"

"You bet you can," said Peter. "But remember," Cindy said to Hope, "you will have to stay on your diet okay?"

"Okay Mom," said Hope.

"We will see you Grandpa and Grandma next week!" The twins gave them a big hug and said goodnight.

"Now," said Cindy, "it is time for you to put pajamas on and get ready for bed. First Hope, you need to eat and have some milk."

The twins got ready for bed and Hope took her milk and ate a little bit of corn flakes. Of course she had to use her special milk with it.

"Can I have some?" said George.

"Sure you can," said Cindy.

When they had finished, Peter said, "alright let's go to bed now. You need your sleep, but let's say our prayers first."

The family said it together and the twins said, "God Bless grandpa and grandma, and Mom and Dad. Amen."

"Very nice, thank you. God loves you."

"Goodnight little one," said Peter and Cindy as they left the twins' room.

Cindy said, "we are the luckiest ones to have beautiful children, and two wonderful parents."

"We definitely are," said Peter.

"As they say, God has our lives planned for us even before we are born. Otherwise, how could we do this without him?"

The next morning, Cindy took the twins to school while Peter went to the church to do some work and had a meeting with some new members. They were the new neighbors his Dad had asked about him about. They did not belong to a church before, but were encouraged by some of the other neighbors. They had two children, also one was in the twins' class. Peter introduced himself as the Pastor and welcomed them to the church.

"I understand your family would like to join the church?"

"Yes Sir," said Mr. and Mrs. Rodger Marsh. "My name is Rodger, and my wife's name is Debbie."

"And who are these lovely little ones?" asked Peter.

"The little girl is Jenny, and this is Paul," said Debbie.

"Well I'm glad to meet all of you. I have two children, also," said Peter. "They are twins and a handful too. Our little girl, Hope, is on a special diet, and little George is so full of energy but a good boy. He is very loving!"

"Well," said Peter, "tell me where you live, and if you're sure you want to join? We are glad to receive new members and help our neighbors all we can."

Rodger told Peter where they live and was sure they would like to join the church. They were very pleasant people and welcome to anything Peter could help them with. Peter talked to them and asked them if their children had been baptized yet.

"No, Pastor." said Debbie.

"Would you like me to have them baptized next Monday?" asked Peter.

"We would like that very much," replied Rodger. "Where we live we didn't attend church because we didn't know anyone, and there wasn't a church close by. So we would be happy to have them baptized on Sunday."

They shook hands and were pleased to meet each other.

Peter said, "Welcome to our church."

Peter was glad to know them and show them God. He finished his meeting and then went to the boys school to see what he could do for his

Dad and the boys. Would that meeting go as well as the one he just left? When Peter arrived at the school, George was the with the boys doing an activity, and the boys who knew Peter stopped and said hello.

George said, "boys, some of you have met Peter, so we will introduce him to our new friends."

George let the older of the boys leave the others to continue their activities while Peter and he went to talk and meet with the one before meeting Mark - the one boy that wouldn't be part of the group. George explained a little to Peter about him.

"He's very hostile, Peter" said George, "he has a background of running away from home. He doesn't seem to want to talk to anyone. That is why I asked you to see if you can get through to him."

"I will see what I can do, Dad. Sometimes a stranger can reach a child, and sometimes not, but I will certainly try. Let's go see the young man," Peter replied.

"Yes sir," said George and they went to Mark's room, only to find out he had left and no one knew he was missing.

"Peter, he is gone," said George. "We need to check the office and the building."

They both looked all over and had asked the boys if they had seen Mark.

"No, Sir." they answered.

George said, "we must call the police department. I hope he is okay! He hasn't done this since he came."

"Does he have any parents?" Peter asked.

"Yes, we should call them. Maybe they would have some idea where Mark would have gone."

Peter thought of the young boy that ran away because his parents didn't love him and said, "Dad maybe we better look at the bus station or on the streets."

"You are right, Son," George answered. "That's a good idea. One of us will have to stay here. Peter, why don't you go. He won't recognize you, and here's a picture of him. We will be praying for him, okay?"

Peter took the picture with him and stopped several people to ask if they saw this young man. He had no luck until he saw a couple of boys playing catch and stopped to talk to them.

"Have you seen this boy?"

"No sir," one replied.

"Are you sure?" asked Peter.

"Mr.," said the other one, "there was a boy that

went into the church over there. He was crying like he was lost."

"Thank you, son." Peter said.

Peter drove over to the church, which was an old one that had a small congregation. Peter went in and saw the young boy sitting by himself - lonely and troubled. He walked up to the boy and asked, "Are you Mark Asher?"

Looking up at him, "why do you ask?" the lad asked.

"Because I thought I could keep you company for a while, if you don't mind." said Peter.

"What if I do?" said Mark.

"Well then I will leave, okay?" Said Peter. "I guess you want to be alone."

As Peter walked away, Mark turned and said, "Wait I do want to talk to someone. Please come back," with a broken sound in his voice.

Peter walked back and sat down by Mark. They were both quiet for a while. Finally Mark asked Peter, "why are you here? Are you lost too?"

"No, Son. I am looking for a young man that left my Dad's school and he is very worried! He asked me to help find this young man." said Peter.

"So you didn't come to talk did you?"

Mark seemed distant but asked, "who are you

and how do you think you can help?"

"My name is Peter, my father is the owner of the Christian school for boys who need guidance."

"No one can help me. No one cares what happens to me," Mark said.

"Why do you say that?" asked Peter.

"Never mind. You don't care. No one cares. Especially my Mom."

"Mark, what happened with your Mom and Dad?" asked Peter.

"It's not your problem." said Mark.

"You know if you talked about it, and get it out of your system, it will help you feel a lot better. You might get rid of some of the anger in you," Peter told him.

"Why do you care?" Mark asked. "You don't even know me."

"No, I don't know you. But I would be glad to listen, and just maybe the two of us can help each other." Peter replied. "Let me tell you something about me. I love my parents so much. They did so much for me. We lived in an old drafty house and my Dad worked in a coal mine and died of Legionnaires disease. My mother died a few years later, leaving me to find my own way. I was only 12 years old. I walked the streets looking for small jobs for food. I had to quit school to find work. I found myself weak and lonely. One night, I was walking on the streets alone. No place to go, and no food. I passed out on the street and when I awoke the next morning, there was a tall nice looking man standing by my bed. I asked him who he was and where I was. He told me he found me on the sidewalk passed out, so he took me to the hospital. I knew then that there were people, even strangers, who care about others. So if you want to talk I'm here to listen. There are angels all around us watching over us. We all have an angel. Even you Mark. So how about telling me about your Mom?

"My Dad passed away last year. I was left alone quite a bit. Mom had to work, and then she wouldn't come home. She started drinking and I couldn't help her, so I ran away to see if she would care. And she didn't even miss me until a week later when she realized I was gone. Then she started worrying and told the cops she couldn't take care of me anymore. So that's why I'm at the Christian School."

"Is she still around Mark?" Asked Peter.

"I guess, but she doesn't care. I told you no one cared," said Mark as tears ran down his cheeks.

Peter put his arms around Mark and embraced him. "It's alright, Son. We do care, and so does God. And you know that because you are here in his house. Mark would you like to see your mother?"

"Sure, but I guess she doesn't want to see me."

"If I can get help for her and bring her to see you, would that be okay?" asked Peter.

"But how can you do that?"

"I am a minister, Mark. I help people in need and who want it."

Peter and Mark talked for quite a while, and then Mark agreed to go back to the boys home. He was sad but he was counting on Peter to help his Mom. When they got back to the home George was waiting for them. "Oh thank God Peter, you found him?"

"Yes, Dad. Mark and I had a long talk. Didn't we Mark?" asked Peter. "Mark do you remember me telling you of a tall nice man finding me?"

"Yes, Sir," said Mark.

"Well Mr. Watkins is him, and now he is my father. He has helped me to grow and become a Minister and a father myself. So you see, there are people that care."

"Wow!" said Mark. "I guess there are. I'm

sorry Mr. Watkins that I worried you. I didn't think anyone would miss me."

"Oh Mark," said George, "of course we miss you. We were very worried, but we are so glad you're back and safe."

It was supper time when Peter and Mark returned to the home, so George asked Mark if he would like some supper and asked the person in charge to take Mark with him.

Mark said, "thank you Peter! I hope we can talk again."

"You bet we can," replied Peter. He said goodnight to mark.

George stayed for a while to see that Mark was okay, then along with Peter they left to go home to their families.

"Where did you find him?" said George.

"In a church a little ways down the road. He was very unhappy. He wants to see his mother, but he doesn't think she wants to see him. So we need to find her and help them come together. Dad, do you remember the new neighbors you asked me about a few weeks ago?"

"Yes I sure do," replied George. "How did you happen to think of them?"

"Well I had a meeting with them before I

came over here to see you. They are joining our church next Sunday, and the two children are to be baptized. Seems like they didn't have a church before."

"What are their names?" asked George.

"Mr. and Mrs. Rodger Marsh. They are very nice people. I know you will like them. They have two children." Peter explained.

"We'll have to make them feel welcome Peter," said George. "Also, I would like to bring Mark with Lynda and I until we can find his mother and help her get back on her feet with some counseling. Mark will need someone to give him a little attention. Then he can help his friend Billy, how does that sound to you Peter?" asked George.

"I think that's a wonderful idea. Sometimes just showing them that we do care makes a big difference," Peter answered.

"He will like that."

"Well Dad, I need to go home and see how Hope and Cindy are doing, so I will see you tomorrow to see how Mark is doing."

"Okay, Son. You have a good night, and thank you so much for finding our lost lamb. And give the twins a hug for mother and me." And they parted to go home.

When Peter got home, he gave the twins a big hug and got them on his lap and asked them how their day at school was, as he usually did. Anxious to see Daddy, they got their school papers and said, "Daddy, look what I did in school," said Little George as Hope showed her Dad.

"I am proud of my little angels, that is so good. Did you drink your milk and eat?" asked Peter.

"Yes," answered Hope.

"Where is Mom?" he asked.

"Making supper," said Georgie.

Peter and the twins went to see Cindy and gave her a hug and said, "that smells good dear."

Cindy said, "what did your Dad have a problem with?"

Peter told Cindy that one of the boys ran away and wanted to ask me to help the young boy.

"Is he okay?" asked Cindy.

"He's going to be fine. Some children growing up in broken homes feel unwanted and need us to let them know others do care and pray for them," he said.

"I'm sorry to hear," that Cindy replied. "Is there anything we can do for him?" she asked.

"Well, Mom and Dad are going to bring him to church Sunday. We also have new neighbors that are joining our church on Sunday, the two children will be baptized. Also, you will get to meet them on Sunday."

"That will be nice," Cindy said as they sat down for supper and all talked about their day and thanked God for their blessings.

"Cindy, would you and Mom mind having the neighbors over for supper on Sunday?" asked Peter.

"I would love to, and I am sure your mother will help and be glad to do it. But I will call her and ask, okay?"

"Great. I'll ask the Marsh's, and Dad can bring Mark - the young boy that is coming to church with them on Sunday."

And George went to get Mark at the boys school, but to their surprise, Mark had a surprise visitor. George asked where Mark was. "He is in with the other boys." The day supervisor replied, "he had a visitor early this morning."

"Who was it? Mark never has company, he's alone except... except it can't be." said George. "It isn't his mother is it?"

"She said she was," replied the supervisor. He wasn't sure he told George, so he let her in to see him.

"Are they here?" asked George.

"They're in Mark's room. I'm sorry if I did something wrong Mr. Watkins."

"Well let's go see Mark, and we'll discuss this later." said George. "Mark was going to church with us today."

They went to Mark's room and were surprised to see a nice looking lady talking to him. She was crying and was saying she couldn't afford to take him home with her. "Why not?" asked Mark ,as he walked over by George with tears in his eyes and George gave him a hug.

"Mark is this your mother?" asked George.

"Yes sir," Mark replied.

"I am Mrs. Charles Daily, Sir. Mark's mother."

George shook hands with her and explained that Mark was going to go to church with them and then to their house for dinner. He looked at her and asked, "would you like to join us Mrs. Daily?"

"I... I don't think so Sir. I need to be at work soon, but maybe another time, thank you."

"But Mom! Why not?" said Mark.

"I'm sorry, Son." she replied. "I have to go now, but I will keep in touch okay?"

As she kissed Mark on the cheek, Mark moved

away and said, "You will never be back, I know you won't."

She left and George and Mark went to church. Peter asked, "Dad, why are you late? Did something happen, is everything okay at the school?"

"Yes Peter," George replied, "everything will be fine. I will let Mark explain after church okay?"

"Sure," said Peter, "but I must go and give the sermon. It is going to be a special day."

Peter put his robe on and went up to see the new family that was to join, and the young one to become a child of God. Cindy and the twins waited for Peter's parents and sat next to the Marshes and introduced themselves to one another. George and Lynda sat next to them, and introduced Mark to them, who was looking very sad.

Cindy had invited all of them to the house after church, and Mark was about the age of the neighbor's son Paul, so they got along well. And the twins had fun playing outside with new friends. Hope and Jenny shared their ideas and toys and became good friends, as Mark and Paul and Little George did. As it was time to return to the home, Mark asked, "do I have to go? Can't

I stay with you and Mrs. Watkins until morning please?"

George and Lynda said to Mark, "don't you think Billy would be sad if he has to be alone? Maybe next time, okay? We will let Billy know, and then he won't wonder where you are. Will that be okay tomorrow?" Asked the Watkins.

"Okay!" Mark was so excited, "I will tell Billy," he said. "I had lots of fun, thank you."

Mark was a boy who can make friends easily. As they arrived at the school, the Watkins walked Mark to his room. They said hi to Billy and gave Mark a hug goodbye. "I hope you enjoyed your day," George said.

"I sure did," he said. "Thank you for taking me, I will help Billy and he will also be okay."

"Well, we will see you tomorrow Mark and Billy, good night!"

The Watkins left to return home, and knew that Mark was going to be okay but still wanted to contact his mother so they could bring the family together and Mark could see his Mom. Where would he start? George wondered, and what would he say? Mark's mother was a good-looking lady, but her parents live far from her and Mark. She worked at a bar at night and part-time at a diner in the afternoon. When George and Peter started looking for her, they asked Mark if he knew where his mother worked or lived so they went to see Mark first. As they arrived in the morning they saw Mark and asked him, "Mark do you know where your mother works? Peter and I want to go help her if we can, so if you know maybe we can go talk to her."

"I'm not sure. It's some bar downtown, but I don't know the name of it. She works at a restaurant in the afternoon that's why she can't take me home," said Mark. "Anyway, I don't want to go home. She's never there and I like it here," he continued.

"Mark, we're glad you like it here and we love having you, but we want to help her so she doesn't hurt herself by drinking and driving. If she knows someone cares, maybe she can change and will come and see you more often, and then you can visit her on weekends. How would you like that?" they asked.

"I guess it's okay, but I don't know where she works," replied Mark, "she didn't tell me."

"Well we can ask around and see if anyone knows her," said Peter.

"So you and Billy have a good time and we will see you later." George said.

"Okay," Mark said, "we will." And he said goodbye to Peter and George.

Finding Mark's mother was going to be a hard thing to do, but George and Peter were determined to help Mark get his family back. The next day, they went to the school and had a staff meeting. Everyone was asked to keep their eyes open for Mrs. Daily. If they saw Mark's mother, they were asked not to say anything to Mark, and no one is to see him without our permission. So George gave them a picture that Mark had, and asked them to keep their eyes open and to call them if they had any information on her.

"We thank you all for coming and helping us," said George. "And we will see you tomorrow."

When George got home, Lynda asked him if he found anything about Mark's mother.

"No dear," he said. "We are giving some pictures out to the staff, and they are going to keep an eye out for her. I am sure we will find her ,but will she want her help? Mark said she has two jobs and one is at a bar at night. I hope we can get her into AA and a different job, so Mark will be able to spend a few days with her. He's a very good boy isn't he?"

"Yes he is. And it would be great to see his Mom

and have a time of joy and happiness together," said Lynda. "If I can help let me know okay?"

"I sure will Lynda, thank you for offering," George replied.

The search started the next day when Peter stopped for a cup of coffee before going to the church office. There was a clerk behind the counter and Peter asked him if he knew the lady in the picture, but the clerk answered, "No sir, I never saw her here. She is very nice looking."

"Well," said Peter, "if you see her, will you contact this number at the school?" He wrote down the number and gave it to the clerk and thanked him.

After finishing his coffee, he went to the church to do some work, but George was still out looking for Mrs. Daily and wouldn't give up. They continued to search for her for several weeks, until one night after Peter and George were coming home from the school, they drove slowly by the downtown restaurant on Main Street and saw lady getting in her car, but was having trouble getting her car started. They walked over to her and took the picture out to look at, and then looked at each other smiling, and knew they had gotten a sign from God. When they got to the car, they knocked on her window to ask if they could help. Suddenly Mrs. Daily recognized George.

She got out of the car and said, "aren't you Mr. Watkins from the Christian boys school?"

"Yes we are," they replied. "I saw you having trouble with your car, and stopped to see if we could help. What seems to be wrong?"

"I don't know, Sir," she said. "It just will not start. I was going to my second job but I guess I will have to walk there, Mrs. Daily said.

Peter said, "may I give you a ride? It is a little cold out and you have no coat on, so if it is alright, I will be glad to give you a ride."

Peter thought this would be a good way to find out where she was working.

"Oh thank you, that would be very nice I appreciate it." she replied.

"You are welcome," said Peter.

When Peter dropped her off, he waited to see where she went and he noticed she had gone into the Friendly Bar but didn't do anything and went back to help his Dad with the car.

"Dad, did you get it started? Will it be ready to take her by the time she gets done working?"

"Yes Peter, I got it started. She had flooded it, so that is why it wouldn't start but it is okay now.

We will take it to her work so she has the keys and will be able to drive home when she is done with work. I bet you are tired aren't you, Peter?" He asked.

"Yes. But I guess you are also. So let's drop her car off and go home to our families. We will find out tomorrow where she lives okay?"

So they returned the car to Mrs. Daily's place of work and hoped that everything would be okay for her. George gave her his number to call if she needed any help, and she thanked them both as they left to go home. George dropped Peter off and waited until he was safely in the house and returned home to find Lynda still waiting up for him. They would always wait up until the other one was home safe.

"Dear, are you still up? It is quite late!"

"Yes George, you know we don't go to sleep unless we are both home. Did you find out anything with Mark's mother? Is she okay?"

"Yes we found out where she works at night, it's called The Friendly Bar, and she couldn't get her car started. So Peter took her to work while I worked on the car. She seems like a very nice person, but I wish she had a different place to work. After Mark's Dad died, she started drinking too much. I know she loves her son, if we can just get her some help so she would spend more time with him but we will work on it. And now we are going to get some sleep. Come on, let's leave God to take care of it tonight," and they agreed on that.

Meanwhile, back at Peter's home, Cindy also waited up wondering and praying that everything was all right. When Peter walked in, Cindy asked Peter if everything was all right. "The children didn't want to go to bed until you came home, so I let them stay downstairs with me."

"Everything is fine dear, I'm sorry it's a little late, but we found out where Mark's mother works at night, she ran into car trouble. Her car wouldn't start that's how we found her. But everything will be okay. We will pray for her and try to get her help so Mark can see her more often."

Peter was tired and had a busy day coming up, so they carried the twins upstairs and tucked them in and he and Cindy said good night.

When they all arose the next morning, it was raining and storming as they looked out the window to see the dark clouds and heavy winds.

"It looks like a bad storm Daddy," said little George. "Can we go play in the rain?"

As Peter was growing up he loved to go run outside in the rain and splash in the puddles, but this was not the type of rain to be going outside as this was going to be a bad storm. So he said to Georgie, "no Son, you cannot, the wind's too strong."

Georgie was disappointed but said, "okay Daddy. Why is it so dark out? Should we turn the lights on?"

"Yes George, you can do that for me while Dad and I close the windows. And Georgie, tell Hope to come down right away." Cindy explained, "we need to take cover so hurry."

Georgie and Hope ran over by Cindy and were scared. They hung tight to their parents until the storm was over, it was a bad one. Peter's house was not damaged, but the house's nearby were. They had roofs torn off and windows broken, also trees were down. When the storm let up, Peter told the twins it was okay and he said a prayer for those who lost their homes, and those who had damage. Then he called his father to see if they were at the school. He was very worried about his Mom Lynda, also hoping she wasn't alone. So when he called George, he asked if Lynda was by herself.

"No," said George, "she is with me. We got all the children down in the storm cellar. Your Mom helped us. So thank God everything is alright, thanks be to God," said George.

"Okay, Dad. Some neighbors had quite a bit of damage, so the church will have to meet and see how we can help," Peter told his Dad. "Dad when you get home call us and let me know how everything is at your house, will you?"

"Sure son, as soon as we get home. How are the children Peter?"

"They were very frightened, but they are fine now," replied Peter.

When George got home and checked things out - the house is fine, but they had lost a beautiful maple tree in the backyard.

"Oh George!" Lynda said, "look the tree we planted years ago got struck down. I'm so glad it didn't hit the house!"

"I'm sorry darling," George said. "It was so beautiful in the fall wasn't it? Well we will have to clean up in the morning, so let's grab a bite to eat. I'm hungry aren't you?" He asked.

"I sure am," she answered.

George told Lynda he was meeting Peter and some other church members of the board to see what they could do to help the storm victims.

"That's a good idea, George" she continued to ask him if there was something she could do to help.

"Well maybe you can call some of Peter's neighbors and see if they need help," George said.

"Okay dear," she said. After they finished lunch they retired to the family room and watched the news to see where all the damage was. It was a small town and everyone joined together to help those in need. It is a very close-knit town that's what Christians do.

At the meeting, Peter and the board met with a prayer first to see what God would have them do. They all worked together to clean the town off and put families together. "It was a bad storm," said Peter, "and we all need help where it is needed. We will ask the congregation to bring food and clothing and supplies for small children."

The board members agreed to help and let people know. When Sunday services came to the church, it was full of people who cared and talked about the storm. Peter gave the sermon as usual and then made the announcement.

"There is an announcement that we need to ask the congregation, so I'm going to let Steve Johnson, our chairman of the board, talk to you."

Steve started by saying, "we are all concerned about this bad storm we had, and the damage that was done. And we know it has been very hard on some of our members. So we would like all of you who can help one way or another please sign up. One is to deliver food or clothing, and the other is to help with the buildings to get them back in shape. There are many ways you can help: donating clothing, and your time. So if you can help, we will be glad to have all of you."

"Thank you all," he said, "we will appreciate it now here is Peter."

"Thank you, Steve." Peter said, "Now let's sing our closing hymn."

After service, many got together to see who and how they could help get their family settled in their homes. Everyone worked for weeks until the town people were back to normal again. George was still trying to find out where Mrs. Daily lived, but had no luck until the night he and Peter waited until she got out of work at the bar, and saw her leave. So they decided to follow her far enough behind so as not to scare her. When she arrived home, they waited a few minutes.

"Well Dad," said Peter, "are we going in or should we take the address down and return tomorrow?"

"We can come back tomorrow," George replied. "She is probably tired and will not feel like talking, okay?"

"Sure, Dad." replied Peter. "We can stop there on your way to the school? How is Mark doing Dad?"

"He is okay. Better than he was, but wanted to know when you were going to see him".

"Well why don't I pick him up in the morning after we stop at his Mom's house? Do you think that would be all right?" Peter asked.

"Or maybe we better go together first and see what her place is like," answered George. "It may not be a place Mark should see."

"All right Dad, that's a good idea."

George drove Peter home and told him he would meet him at his house at 9 a.m. to go visit Mrs. Daily.

"Okay, Dad. That sounds good, so I will see you in the morning at 9 a.m. Thanks Dad goodnight."

Peter joined his family in prayer before bedtime. He and Cindy sat quietly by the fireplace while they read to the twins, and Hope and Little George sat on Dad's lap and showed Peter what they did in Sunday school, and sang a song they have learned.

"Did you like that Dad?" they asked.

"It was beautiful. Now it is time for bed because you have school in the morning. So let's go, okay? Say your prayers, Mommy and I will listen."

As they finished, Peter and Cindy kissed them goodnight and went to the fireplace and sat and talked.

"Cindy, how would you like to go on vacation? We haven't had one for a long time have we?"

"No Peter, we haven't and I think that's a wonderful idea. When?"

"Well I don't know yet, I need to make plans for someone to cover for me while I'm gone."

"What about the children? Will they go with us?" asked Cindy.

"Sure dear, we will wait until they have a school vacation. They are our family, we can't leave them out Peter. It will be fun for them, also."

It was also near the spring break and Cindy said she would check on the schedule and then she could let Peter know.

"It is going to be so exciting Peter! Where

would we go? There are so many places to see. Oh Peter, it will be great won't it? We will have fun relaxing on a beach in Florida."

"We have never been to Disneyland or Florida. That will be great for the twins don't you think?" asked Peter.

"I'm sure they will love it," replied Cindy. "We also need to talk to Mom and Dad don't we?"

"Yes indeed, we will discuss it with them tomorrow okay? Dad will be able to handle the school. He's very good at that and has a reliable worker. Also Mom will help him. They will be fine."

But then Peter got to thinking about Mark at the school and that he has to stop and see his mother in the morning with his Dad so he said to Cindy, "I need to meet with Dad in the morning to see Mrs. Daily."

"Who is Mrs. Dailey?" asked Cindy.

"She is Mark's mother," Peter replied, "and we followed her home the other night, and we want to see what kind of place she lives in before we tell Mark. Would you and Mom like to come along dear?"

Cindy thought for a minute and said, "I don't think it would be a good idea Peter, at least not the first time. She may not feel comfortable with so many. Does she know you and Dad are coming?"

"No dear, if we tell her she may not answer her door and we may not get to see her and how she lives and Mark would be unhappy. So we'll take it slow and cautious."

The following day, George picked Peter up and they left to go see how they could help Mark's mother and to see if it was a place Mark would be happy in. As they reached Mrs. Daily's place, they decided Peter being a pastor of the church would be the spokesperson and introduce George again, although Mrs. Daily had remembered him. They approached her door and rang the doorbell. It was a while before she opened the door, until she saw Peter because he was the one who drove her to work the night her car was stalled.

When she opened the door she greeted them in and they said, "I hope this isn't a bad time to see you Mrs. Daily?"

"No, please come in." She was very pleasant and offered them a cup of coffee. "What can I do for you? Is Mark okay?" she asked sounding very concerned.

"Well that's why we came to talk to you. About letting Mark come home on weekends so you and your son can spend some quality time together," said George. "Did you know your son ran away a few weeks ago?" he asked.

"No, I'm sorry. Why did he do that?" asked Mrs. Daily. "He knows I work, he is okay?" she asked George. She seemed quite worried.

"He is fine," said Peter. "I found him in a little church down the street, he was sitting by himself crying and very lonesome."

Peter continued to tell Mark's mother what he talked about, and that Mark said she didn't care about him and that Mark and him had become friends - someone he could talk to.

"Well what can I do to help? I miss him too, but I have to work. I sleep on the couch, where would my son sleep? Don't you see, it is not a place I could bring my son home to is it? He is better off at the school with boys his age and I'm frustrated," she said. "I don't know what to do."

"Wait, Mrs. Daily. What days do you have off?" Trying to get some idea how to get them together asked Peter. She told them she only has one day off a week and that days she spends it cleaning and doing errands.

"Maybe... maybe," said George, "we can have you and Mark join us for supper on the day you're off, so you can get to know your son and let Mark understand this. At least visit him once a week and let him know you care and you still love him. He needs to know this from you."

"All right." she agreed. "You set up the time and place and let me know. After Mark's Dad died I couldn't take care of him and work too, and I thought he would be better off at the school where he got care and love!"

"Well I think visiting will help," said George. "Don't you, Peter?"

"Yes I do," said Peter. "Mark wants me to stop and see him today so I will talk to him and let him know. I'm sure he will be happy to hear it. But Mrs. Daily, you need to let us know what day you have off before we can set up a time for our meeting. How was your car? If you need a ride, Mr. Watkins can pick you up when he brings Mark. But let us know what day is good for you."

She smiled and said she would as soon as she could. "Thank you both for coming and caring for Mark," then she said goodbye.

As George and Peter left for their daily commitments, they talked about getting Mrs.

Daily a different place to live and a job she could enjoy and not work at two jobs. She should be home at night with Mark. Mark is 12 years old, he would be in school in the daytime and his mother can pick him up after she got done with work. In the summer time he can stay at the school in the day. They stopped at the school. George went into his office to take care of things.

"Peter," said George, "would you like to talk to Mark? I think they are at activities."

"That would be a good time," Peter replied.

They went to get Mark and noticed he wasn't enjoying himself, he was sitting alone.

"Mark!" George called.

Mark looked up and began to smile because he had seen Peter. He walked over by them and George asked him, "Mark, would you like to go with Peter? He has something to talk to you about."

Mark said, "sure Mr. Watkins. Where are we going, Peter?" he asked.

"Where would you like to go?" asked Peter. "You pick the place."

"Can we go to the park and watch the squirrels and just sit and talk?"

"That sounds like a nice place," said Peter.

As they left Peter said, "we will be back in a little while Dad."

When Mark heard Peter say Dad, he thought how nice it would be to have his Dad around. Peter and Mark were quiet in the car as they were driving to the park. When they got there they saw some geese walking around. "Can we feed the geese?" asked Mark. "Look there are so many of them. Can we Peter?"

"Well maybe later, we don't have anything to feed them with." replied Peter. "I guess everyone feeds them, see they get plenty to eat. It won't be long and they will be flying south where it is warmer. Come on Mark, let's sit and talk okay?"

"About what, Peter?"

"About your Mom. Let's talk about your Mom."

"Okay," excited and full of smiles. "So what about my Mom? Am I going to see her? Am I?"

"I hope so," said Peter. "We are trying to find your mother a good job and a bigger place to live so you can live with her. Would you like that?" asked Peter.

"I... I don't know. I'm not sure she wants me too," Mark said.

"Of course she does," Peter said. "She misses you very much, she said she does. But she just doesn't have an extra room and cannot afford a lot of things boys need."

"I don't need a lot Peter, I just want mother to love me, and we can visit Dad at the cemetery and talk together and go to church together. Don't you see Peter, I just want to see and be with her. She needs me. I know she does!"

"Well you are right about that, so my father Mr. Watkins and I, will try and work together to get you and your mother back together okay? But it will take some time. So cheer up and soon you will be home with your mother. Only one thing Mark."

"What's that asked Mark?"

"You will be at the Christian school during the day while your mother is working okay?" said Peter.

"Okay!" Mark smiled and gave Peter a big hug with tears in his eyes and a smile on Peters face so happy to see Mark excited and smiling again.

"Okay, we need to get back to the school with the other boys. They aren't as lucky as you. Some of them have no one at all. So we need to ask God to help them right?" Said Peter.

Mark agreed and he and Peter drove back to the school and Mark joined the other boys in their activities as Peter talked to George and returned to his church to attend his duties there, and to start searching for a new home for Mark and his mother.

Sunday morning worship was to be an exciting one, a child was born to save us all. It was Christmas Eve and everyone was singing carols and exchanging gifts at home that night. Peter gave a sermon on Jesus being born in a stall - many did not know what a stall was, they always heard it was called a Manger. But actually, a stall is a bed made up of straw and hay in a barn where Mary and Joseph gave birth to Jesus. And as he was talking, he remembered and said, "we have a family in town that needs a home so they can be together again. This family lost her husband, and her son lost his father. So like Jesus, they keep looking for a place so they can be together. This is what it is all about isn't it?" Peter said.

For a moment it was quiet and everyone wondered how they could help. "So this Christmas I am going to ask you all to bow your heads and ask yourselves, how can I help God?"

Suddenly, Peter said, "if anyone knows of a home that may be rented or lived in, you may call my office or home at any time. But there is another way you may help this family. The mother needs a job, full-time." Peter said. "So her son can live with her again. We will take a special collection for them for Christmas, for those who wish to give. Thank you for all your prayers, and I know this will be a blessed Christmas to all."

They sang :Go Tell It on the Mountain" and closed the services. It was a friendly church and many of them waited to talk to Pastor Peter at the end of the sermon with greetings and wishing all a merry Christmas. Peter met with those who stayed after and it was a pleasant time for all who stayed.

Peter was sure he had reached the people that night on Christmas Eve about giving themselves and knowing what it meant - about a child and his mother needing a home as a baby Jesus did to keep him from harm that night. Peter had received many calls that next week some included a new job for Mrs. Daily, and some called about a vacancy in an apartment. George and Peters family went together to see the places, and we're very pleased with the response of the congregation. They had collected enough for the mother and sons' first three months rent to get her started, and had found a pleasant home for Mark and his mother. They took Mark and his Mom to see it together.

George said to Mark the next day, "we have a surprise for you Mark. Peter and I want to take you and your mother for a ride tomorrow. So you get a good night's sleep, and we will see you in the morning okay?"

"Sure," said Mark. "But where are we going?"

"You will have to wait and see, it is a surprise," Peter said.

Mark said okay and then went to his room and got ready for bed, but was curious and had a hard time getting to sleep that night. He was saying his prayers and fell asleep.

The following morning Lynda and Cindy got up early and got the children off to school, and was anxious to go with George and Peter. But they would have to take separate cars because George and Peter had to pick up Mark and Mrs. Daily, but they didn't mind because they just wanted to help wherever they could. When they all reached Mrs. Daily's place, Peter got out with his Dad they walked up to the house and rang her doorbell g- lad to find her at home. Peter motioned to Cindy and his Mom to come in. Mrs. Daily opened the door and was very surprised to see George and Peter.

"Is something wrong?" she asked. She didn't know why they were all there.

"No, no everything is going to be great!" they said. "Mrs. Daily, have you met Cindy and my mother?"

"No, hi. I am glad to meet you both." Said Mrs. Daily."Well what can I do for you all?"

"Well," said Peter, "you can put on your coat and we are going to pick up Mark and we are all going to go for a ride, so grab your coat okay?"

Mrs. Daily got her coat and got in the car, anxious to see Mark, but what else are they up to? She couldn't figure that one out, so she sat quietly until they picked up Mark, gave him a big hug and said she was happy to see him.

"I'm glad to see you too, Mom." Replied Mark, "where are we going Peter?"

"You will see it in a little while, so wait patiently and you will find out."

As they drove into an area of very nice homes near a park, they pulled up to a small home with a beautiful yard. George and Peter opened the car door.

"What are we doing here?" Mrs. Daily asked.

Cindy and Lynda got out of the car and they all walked up to the house where the owner met them at the door.

"Hello," she said. "You must be the Watkins family. Come in, please. I'm very glad to meet you all. I know Pastor Watkins."

"Hi Mrs. Johnson. Is Ben here?"

"Oh yes," she said and called Ben to the door when they were in and then came and introduced himself to everyone. Mark looked down at the house and said, "what are we doing here?"

"Well," said and Mr. Johnson, "let's all come in and sit down. I'm on the church board and I own a couple of homes, but I am looking for someone to take over one of them. This one is just right for a small family, so Peter if you will explain to Mrs. Daily and Mark, maybe they will understand, okay?"

"Sure!" Said Peter. Peter explained it all to Mark and his Mom. Cindy and Lynda congratulated them, and welcomed them to the neighborhood.

"But I, but..." said Mrs. Daily. "We don't have the money for this house is beautiful. I don't make enough to keep it up, how?"

George and Peter interrupted her and replied, "well we have that taken care of that. Our church congregation took a collection for you, it will get you started and we would also like you to meet your new boss, Mrs. Ben Johnson. He has a job for you and you won't have to work two jobs, we hope you will accept it."

"Well! I I don't know…" said Mrs. Daily. "Can I ask what it is and where?"

"Sure!" The Johnsons explain to her all she wanted to know.

"I don't know how to thank you all. Does this mean Mark will be home with me at night?"

"It sure does," said George. "How do you and Mark feel about that?"

"That's really great," Mark replied. "This is the best Christmas ever!" he said. "Thank you God."

"So," said Mr. and Mrs. Johnson, "when can you move in?" with a happy look on his face.

Mark and his Mom were so happy they were going to be together at last. Now they could see each other every day and tell each other things that happened during their day.

Peter and George helped Mark and his mother move into their new home. Mrs. Daily liked her new job, and Mark and her did all the things he dreamed about doing with his Mom, but still stayed up at school where he grew in faith and he and his mother joined the church that gave them so much help to get back together, and made many new friends.

Peter and Cindy spent Sunday at church in the office making calls to homes that needed a communion and prayers. Those in need enjoyed her company, and liked visiting with her. The church had grown since he had become the Pastor, but now they were thinking of their vacation plans that Peter talked about. The twins would be out of school soon and it was time they spend time together.

Going on Vacation

"Peter, have you thought any more about our vacation? Now that Mark and his mother are doing well, I think we should take time and spend it with the twins."

"Yes dear," Peter said. "I have an associate Pastor to fill in for us during that time. He is very happy to do it. So you and the children will get things together. We will talk to them tomorrow, okay? I know they will be excited. It will be an exciting time."

As they rose the next morning, they all gathered for breakfast and saw the sun shining bright as Peter asked Hope to say the prayers.

"Thank you for our food and our family, and thank you for the light from the sun that shines on us today. Amen."

"That was wonderful, Hope." said Cindy. "Now

Daddy has something he wants to ask you two."

"What is it?" asked Little Georgie, "are we going to move?"

"Oh no, son. Why did you ask that?"

"Because Mark and his Mom moved didn't they?"

"Yes, but they didn't have a nice house and now they can be together. Mark's mother didn't have room for him to live with her in the other house. But we have lots of room, so no we are not moving. But how would you like to go to see Disneyland?"

"Yeah, yes Daddy."

They got up from their chairs and hugged Peter and Cindy. "Thanks Daddy!" they were so happy they forgot about school.

"When can we go?" asked Hope.

"Well," said Peter, "we can go when school is out. And Hope you will have to see your doctor first. So we have about four weeks to get ready okay? Look at the time, you better get to school and I and your Mom have to get to work. So you be good in school and work hard."

It was so exciting to the twins that they got ready to go so they could tell their friends and teachers.

As they prepared for the weeks ahead, Peter and Cindy called his Mom and Dad and told them. George and Lynda would watch the house and take care of the mail for them while they were gone.

"We are so glad you have worked so hard and helped so many people," Lynda told them.

"You sure deserve to go on vacation. Peter, who is filling in for you at church?" asked George.

"Well, Dad. I have asked an associate Pastor, and he was glad to fill in but I wanted to ask you to help with other things if he needs answers or has questions - would you mind?"

"No Son, I would be happy to, so don't worry about anything. God will take care of everything."

As time came close to the vacation, the twins got more excited and looked at pictures of Disney and talked about seeing Mickey and his friends. Hope had gone to the doctor for her checkup, it was an excellent report but to be on the safe side she still had to stay on her diet.

At last, school was out and vacation day was here. Suitcases were packed, but Cindy wondered was the special milk packed? She had better check.

Peter asked her, "do you have any of Hope's special food for her?"

"Yes, Dear." she said, "but check and make sure okay? Maybe the twins better take some game and colors and a book to keep them busy, don't you think so?"

"Oh yes," Peter replied. "That will keep them busy while traveling. That's a good idea."

Peter's Mom and Dad came over early the next morning to see how they could help and to wish them a good trip. George asked Peter, "do you need help with those suitcases?"

He walked over and picked one up. "Wow what have you got in there? I'm not sure what all the family packed but," joking he said, "I hope it's not lead," and he and George laughed.

They continued to load the van that they got because it would be more roomy, and the little ones could sleep better. "Oh Dad, here are the keys to the house and the mailbox okay? I hope you and Mom will be okay. We will miss you both."

Cindy and Lynda got the twins and were ready to get them settled in the van when Hope said, "Grandma, I need you to go to the restroom can you take me?"

"Sure come on, Grandma will take you. Little George do you need to go?" she asked. "It's a long drive."

Little George got out and went with them while Peter and Cindy talked to George.

"We will call you when we get settled at the hotel Dad," they said.

When Hope and Little Georgie returned, they gave Grandpa and Grandma a big hug and said, "I wish you were coming too."

"Well maybe next time okay?" Said Grandma and Grandpa. "You and your parents have a good time and shake hands with Mickey."

And they all climbed in the van and were ready to go, waving goodbye to each other.

George and Lynda watched until they were out of sight and went back into the house to make sure lights and everything was off. Looking around Lynda said to George, "it is so quiet. I miss them already. I hope they drive carefully."

"Peter will, Dear." he said. And, "Yes, I miss them already too. But I'm glad they have a chance to go and be together. I am sure they will have fun. Come on Dear, let's lock up and go get something to eat. I am hungry aren't you?? George asked Lynda.

"I sure am," she replied.

As they were on their way home, they stopped at the school to make sure everything was going fine. John and Jerry had come back from college to see the Watkins' and Peter. George and Lynda were glad to see that they were so grown up. George shook hands with them and asked them if they would like to join them for lunch.

"We are going to stop to eat," he said, "and we would be glad to have you join us."

"We would love to," the boys said. "We have had a long ride, and now we are getting to see our good friends and teacher this is great."

"We thought we would get to see Peter."

"Peter and the family are in Disneyland on vacation with the twins," said Lynda. "But I am sure he would be so happy to see you both. How long will you boys be here?"

"Well, we're not sure. We thought we would look for some work down here and if we like it we would stick around for a while. We only have one year of college left, and then we might join the Navy."

"Well," said George, "let's go eat and we can talk about it okay?"

The Watkins and John and Jerry found a small quiet place to eat and talk. George told the boys he would ask around and see if he can find a job for them. After they were done eating, George took the boys by John's parents but when he pulled up to the house he said, "Wait boys..."

"Oh thank you Mr. Watkins for lunch it was very nice."

"That's not what I was thinking, I wonder, do you two want to join us at the school this summer? We could use the extra help with school being out. How would you like that?" said George. "Lynda thought she and I could use some time off together."

"Well, may we let you know in the morning?" They started to walk to the house while they Watkins waited to see if they got in okay, but before they got to the door they turned to George and said, "okay we'll take it!" and gave a thumbs up and parted for the day.

George gave the boys a phone number and he and Lynda drove on and stopped at the church to thank God for sending the boys to them and then drove home.

Lynda was reading the paper while George was doing some paperwork, she turned to him and asked, "why don't we go away for the weekend? The two boys and Mr. Clemens are doing fine. They have our number if they have any questions. How does that sound?" she asked.

"That's a good idea," he answered. "Where would you like to go?"

"Well," she replied, "how does just going to the lake cottage and just enjoying the fresh air and the beauty of the sky and sea and go on a boat ride sound? We haven't done that for a long time!"

"That sounds great," George said. "We can go tomorrow and be back when Peter and the family returns home."

They packed and were excited to get away by themselves. Peter had called them to see how his Mom and Dad were, and was glad to hear they were okay. He was happy to hear they were getting away for a few days. They sure deserve it he thought. They had helped Mark and his mother come together, and they were coming along well. The school had responsible workers, and the church came together to help Peter keep things going smoothly. So what else could they have to worry about?

They had a good weekend together at the cottage, and I returned before Peter and the family that night from their two weeks vacation.

Prayers for Hope

On the way home from the airport, Hope started fussing and said to Cindy, "Mommy, I don't feel very good."

Now, Hope was a quiet child, and very seldom complained, but this was different than just a headache. Peter pulled into a station and checked to see if Hope was running a fever.

"Peter, we need to get her to a hospital," said Cindy. "Call mom and have her call the doctor so he can be there okay?"

Peter called his parents and told them to meet them at the hospital.

"Is Hope going to be okay daddy?" asked Little George.

They were able to know when there was something wrong with the other, so Little

George was worried, he said, "should we pray for her, Mommy?"

"Yes sweetie, that would be a good thing."

Hope laid with her head on a pillow, and Peter hurried to the hospital where his mom and dad and the doctor were waiting for them. Lynda and George met them and asked Cindy, "how is she? What happened?"

She was a little scared because she knew Hope couldn't leave them all, she and little George were their pride and joy.

"Bring her in the, doctor's waiting."

"Can I come?" asked Little George.

"No dear." Grandma set him on her lap, and Grandpa gave him a hug and said, "the doctor will take care of her and make her feel better. They will let us know how she is soon, so we will pray for her okay?"

"Okay," said Little George, "but I want to see her when she comes out."

He was very close to his sister. He sat with his grandma and grandpa and almost fell asleep when Peter came out from seeing the doctor.

"How is she Peter?" asked George.

You could see on Peter's face that there was something wrong. "What is it son?" asked Lynda, sounding very worried.

"Well," said Peter, "Hope has a very bad virus - she must have picked it up while we were on vacation. So we need to wait till the doctor takes a test to find out what it is."

"Can she come home, Daddy?" asked Little George.

"No son," Peter replied. "She has to stay here for a few days so the doctor can help her get well again."

"But Daddy, can I stay and see her?" asked Little George.

"No sweetheart," said Peter. "Hope can't have visitors until we know what she has, then Daddy and Mommy will bring you up to see her, okay?"

"Okay Daddy," he said with a frown, "but I hope the doctor can make her well soon so we can see her".

"I am sure he will, but now you can help Hope by taking care of her bunny at home," said Peter.

"Okay, daddy," he said.

At that time, the doctor and Cindy came out. They advised them to go home and get some rest, but Cindy insisted on staying the night. So Peter took Little George, home and George and Lynda went with them and told Peter he should let them know if he needed them.

Peter took Little Georgie home and said goodnight to his parents. Little George helped his dad carry things in from the vacation trip, and they settled down for the night. He gave Georgie a hug and kissed him goodnight. They had had a long trip and a very nice vacation, but it had ended with a serious problem for Hope.

The following morning, Peter and Little George had gone to church to pray for little Hope. They saw the Pastor who filled in for them and explained what happened. Peter thanked him for taking his place and how pleased he was. He told him he was on his way to the hospital, and he couldn't take Georgie, but his Grandma would take good care of him. Georgie loved going by Grandpa, so he didn't get upset about not going with his Dad. He would go with Grandpa to the school, and so he did while Peter relieved Cindy so she could get some food and rest for a while. Hope was asleep and Peter came in and soon the doctor came in and talked to him.

"Peter, good morning. I'm glad you are here," said the Doctor.

Peter said, "good morning, doctor." And asked, "what did you find out? Is she going to be okay?"

The doctor told Peter, "we need to keep Hope for a few days to get her protein back under control. Can you remember," the doctor asked, "what she ate while on vacation other than her diet?"

"No doctor," said Peter. "We watch her very closely why? Is that what is wrong? Please doctor, tell me she is going to be okay. She is, isn't she?" Peter sounded so scared the doctor had to calm him down.

"Yes Peter," the doctor said that she will be fine. "I didn't mean to worry you, but it seems she ate something that was spoiled and it has made her protein go high, and that is what caused her to get sick."

"Will it be okay Doctor?" asked Peter.

"She will need to stay for a few days until we get it regulated. We will keep her as comfortable as possible, and lots of fluids, and she will be fine."

"Thank you doctor, I am glad to hear that." said Peter. "Thank God for watching over her."

"Amen to that," replied the doctor.

"We will see you tomorrow, and I told Hope she can't eat anything for a day except liquids," and he left to see the rest of his patient.

Peter sat next to Hope and saw how weak she looked. Hope looked at him and said, "Daddy, can you stay and read a story to me please?" with a very weak voice.

"Sure darling," he answered. "What would you like to hear me read? How about Cinderella. You have seen it laying on the stand. I will be here as long as I can."

"Okay Daddy," she said as she laid and listened while Peter covered her up and gave her a kiss.

"God bless you sweetie."

He walked the halls while Hope was asleep and happened to see George down the hall. He walked down to meet his dad and told him what the doctor had said and that Hope was going to be okay. They talked for a while and George asked if he could see her, so they walked back up to her room. She was still sleeping, but looks so fragile, but like a little angel.

Peter asked George, "would you like to go to the chapel with me while Hope is sleeping?"

"I would like that very much," he said.

They stopped at the desk and told the nurse where they would be, if Hope should wake up. As they were praying, Cindy came in and prayed with them. Peter got a feeling that he should return to Hopes' room. As they got there, Hope was awake and sitting up crying.

"Hope! What's the matter?" He went over and hugged her.

"Daddy, Mommy - you were gone. I was scared that you went away. I don't want you to go." And then she looked over and saw Grandpa and she gave him a big smile. "Hi Grandpa," she said.

George gave her a hug and asked if it would be okay if he and Grandma stayed with her so that mommy and daddy could get some rest. Hope smiled and said in a quiet voice, "I would like that Grandpa. Where is Grandma?"

"Well, Grandma's watching Georgie. She is coming when Daddy picks Georgie up. She will be here soon, okay? So you get some rest."

Cindy and Peter kissed Hope and said, "we will be back - love you."

As they left, they looked back and was glad Grandpa was there with Hope as he always was for them, from children to adult.

Hope continued to recover and was able to go home in a week, but was to see the doctor a week after she leaves the hospital, and to continue the visits once a month. George was anxious to have his sister come home, so he didn't have to sleep alone.

Peter and his parents were especially happy

that their little angel was going to be alright. They couldn't wait to see Hope run and play with her friends and Little Georgie. Hope recovered and was very good about taking her medicine and doing what the doctor told her she must do. Peter and Cindy continued to watch over Hope, and Georgie was very protective of his sister. Grandpa and Grandma visited her every day. While Hope was home, she continued to play on the keyboard. She liked music, would this be her dream when she grew up? Peter heard her play at times and often wondered, "would this be her goal of life, what is God telling her?"

She probably will be good at playing, what would it be like when they grow up? Would they want to follow in his and Cindy's footsteps, doing God's work, or in another direction? Would Georgie take his Grandpa's place at the school, or would he follow in Peter's footsteps as a Minister? This was something Peter and Cindy had wanted for them.

Peter's dream was to have his children, Hope and George, follow in his footsteps as a Minister spreading the word of God. But Hope had other things in mind while recovering from her illness - she began taking piano lessons.

When she was four, she started playing at a table piano or a child's toy, and Cindy was fascinated at what Hope had picked up and said, "Hope! That was good, where did you learn that?"

Hope replied, "Mom, I was just picking up on it. Did you like it?"

It was a surprise to Cindy that her little girl could pick up notes like that at the age of four. Hope continued each day to pick it up as a toy. Hope's brother George would join in and try helping or interrupting Hope, and Hope would walk away and let George play on it. But to George, it wasn't really fun. He just wanted to see what Hope could play and wanted to try.

Following in Peter's Ministry wasn't what Hope was leaning toward. Little George liked kicking a ball around and is a very rowdy little boy.

"Georgie," his mom would say. "Stop jumping over everything and sit down. Please!"

It would make Cindy feel nervous that her son would get hurt. Georgie was a very active boy. At the age of five he took karate. Peter thought it would help protect himself, but Georgie would get a little too rough at times, and they would have to let him know he had to be more careful. Hope would cry and say, "Mommy! Georgie kicked me."

"George! You must be careful around your little sister," Peter told him.

"Okay Daddy. I'm sorry."

The twins have their own little friends and ideas of having fun.

"Daddy can I go see my little friend and play outside?" asked Little George.

"Sure you can Georgie, but don't play in the roads okay?" answered Peter.

"Okay Dad, I won't do that. I'll play in the yard."

Peter was going to his office to write his sermon for Sunday. He was thinking back when Hope got sick on the way home. "Our little girl. Why did God give her this, why can't he heal her?" All these questions coming at him, why was he punishing God?

He finally woke up from his days and replied to God and said, "he's not to blame. No one is. We can't blame God, he is our protector, and the one true person who can help us. I am sorry. Forgive me please. But there are so many questions I need to have answered forgive me."

So Peter went to church to be alone. "Cindy," he said. "I will be back in a little while okay? I'm going to the church."

"Why Peter?" Cindy asked, "it is quite late isn't it? Can I help?"

"No dear," replied Peter. "I need to be alone for a while, I have something to do."

"Okay," said Cindy. "Let's say goodnight to the children before you go."

Peter went to see the twins when they came in from playing outside. "I'm going to the church for a while, so you to be good for Mommy."

It was about 7 and Peter gave the twins a hug. "I will stop to see you when I get home and kiss you two goodnight! Hope! Remember to eat before you go to sleep promise?"

Because Hope had to eat at certain times and the correct amount of her milk.

"I promise Daddy. Mommy will help, won't you Mommy? Georgie will eat some too," said Hope and gave Peter a big hug.

"Bye Daddy," Georgie said gave Peter a goodbye hug. "See you later dad!"

Cindy kissed Peter goodbye, and then took the twins in to read to them. Peter had something on his mind, she decided to sit the twins down and read to them out of the Bible and they all three pray to God for answers Peter's questions that bothered him, and then got ready for bed.

"Can we wait for Daddy?" asked Hope.

"Yeah can we?" asked Georgie.

"Well for a little while," Cindy said.

They settled down watching a movie and munching on popcorn while waiting for Peter to come home. Meanwhile, the phone rang and when Cindy answered it, it was Grandpa George on the other line. "Hello Cindy," he said, "how are you all?"

"We are fine Dad," she said. "The twins are waiting for Peter to come home."

"Where is Peter?" George asked.

"He has gone to the church to write a sermon for Sunday. But there is something bothering him, I know there is."

"What do you think it is Cindy?" asked George.

"I don't know Grandpa he didn't say. He will probably explain when he gets home." Cindy replied, "I hope it is soon, the twins want to wait up for him."

Well maybe I will take a ride over there to see if I can help him, so don't worry okay?" said George.

"Thank you Dad," she said. That made Cindy feel better. Maybe George could talk to Peter and get some answers.

George went to the church to find Peter praying in the chapel and went and sat by his son and prayed with him. Then he asked, "Peter is something bothering you? Cindy is worried and the twins are waiting up for you. What's wrong son?"

Peter had tears in his eyes, he hasn't cried since his mother died, and George was there then also to help him.

"Dad," Peter said. "What are you doing out so late? I'm glad you're here, I need to talk to someone, especially you."

"What about Peter? Cindy said you came down to write your sermon, but there seems to be something else bothering you."

"Dad! When Hope came home from the hospital, I came to accept the fact that she would have this illness all her life, and not be able to eat what all the other children eat. I started questioning God, but how could this happen? Why, and why my little girl? Why Dad? It is going to be very hard!"

"Peter, Peter remember when your mother was very sick? I mean Mrs. Glennis? And when you didn't know what to do?"

"Yes Dad, I remember. Why do you ask?"

"Well didn't she tell you to be strong, and that God loves you and protects all his children? Even your children?"

"Yes Dad." tears were in his eyes.

"Well he does. You know that he will protect Hope from anything that she has to go through. She also has a good Christian family taking care of her."

"Thanks Dad, I'm glad you came. I am sorry I blamed God for Hope's problem, as she is such a sweet child. Well little George is too, but Hope is our special Angel. Little George is too. I just don't want to lose either one."

"Peter, Hope will be just fine! God will take care of all of her needs. So thank God for her, and know that she is in good hands okay? Did you get your sermon written?" asked George.

"No dad, but I know what it's going to be. Thank you," said Peter to his dad and said, "let's go home."

They both left the church together and felt a relief that they hadn't felt before. They realized that God heard their prayers. "Tell Mom hello," said Peter.

When Peter got home, Cindy was waiting up for him and the twins were asleep. "Peter, are you alright?" asked Cindy. "I was worried about you. Did Dad come down there?"

"Cindy I am fine dear. Yes Dad came down and we had a very nice talk with God."

"What was wrong dear?" Cindy asked.

"Well," Peter replied, "let's check on the twins and get ready for the night, then we will sit by the fire and talk okay?"

"Sure, okay." Cindy said, but was a little puzzled.

After everything was okay for the night, Cindy and Peter sat by the fireplace and talked about Hope, and they knew they had to trust God with whatever came their way. They talked about what was on their mind, and were able to sleep peacefully. The next morning the twins awoke before Peter and Cindy they walked into their parent's room and jumped on their bed.

"Wake up Mommy and Daddy, wake up!" Just as Peter grabbed them and tickled them Cindy woke up.

"Let's all go down for breakfast," she said and they all started tickling her.

"Haha we got you mommy!" The twins pounced on her and she wiggled her way out of that, and they followed her downstairs.

"Come on Daddy," Hope called.

"I'm coming," said Peter and they all went downstairs to have breakfast together while they are still together. That was their important time together as a family.

Before going to the boys school, Lynda and George stopped to see the family, Lynda wanted to see if she could help with the children.

"Cindy can I help with the twins or anything? I would be glad to help and stay with them if you need to go shopping or help Peter?"

The twins saw their Grandma and said, "please Mom, can Grandma stay today?"

They love their grandparents.

"Well I would like to get some errands done, if you don't mind Mom? Peter has a lot to do, so maybe I can go see if I can help him at church. Are you sure Mom?" said Cindy.

"Sure! That's what grandmas are for."

"Yeah!" yelled Georgie and Hope.

"Okay, you to be real good for Grandma," Cindy told them.

"We will be fine," said Lynda. "George will pick me up when he gets done at school, so you go do what you have to do." And she gave Cindy a hug and said goodbye.

"Oh Mom, don't forget Hope's diet!"

"I won't!" said Lynda.

They said goodbye and the twins and their grandma went into the house, and Hope showed her grandma how she could play the piano. It was a tabletop one that her neighbor had given her to play with.

"Hope, that is very good. Someday you will make a great piano player," said Lynda.

"Grandma, I take karate classes," said Georgie, "you want to see me do some kicks?" he asked.

"Sure Georgie. Come on Hope, let's watch George do some of his karate kicks." said Grandma. "Then maybe we can go for a walk and find some pretty leaves outside!"

Hope wasn't anxious to watch Georgie, because he can kick pretty hard, but she sat by Grandma so she didn't get hit. After Georgie did his practice, Lynda checked the clock to make sure she didn't miss Hope's diet time.

"Hope come and get your lunch and milk okay?" Lynda said. "Georgie you come also, and then we will go out for a walk."

"I'm coming," Georgie said. "When is Mommy and Daddy coming home?"

"I don't know sweetie, but let's go for a nice

walk and let's see all the different birds and how many flowers we can find. Would you like that?" asked Lynda.

"Also colored leaves, we can show them to Daddy and Mommy when they come home," the twins said.

While Peter was at the church, Cindy went to his office to see if she could help him with something. "Hi darling," she said. "What are you doing? May I help you? Your mom is with the twins so I thought I would stop to see you after I did my errands."

Peter gave Cindy a hug and was happy to see her. "Well, let me see. There is a new person coming Sunday to join our church. Would you like to stop on the way home and visit her? That would help me very much. But before you go, would you read my sermon and see how or what you think?" asked Peter.

"Sure," said Cindy.

Cindy read the sermon and tears started running down her cheeks. "What's wrong?" asked Peter. "Don't you like it?"

"Oh yes Peter." Cindy said. "It is just the right thing for one like this. It will let the congregation know that not only they need God, but also that

Pastors need him just as much. It's wonderful Peter."

"I'm glad you like it. I was blaming God for Hope's illness, and I was wrong. Dad reminded me what Mother Glennis told me. To be strong in the Lord, and He will give you strength to carry on. So I am glad it is okay ,"he said. "Well I'd better let you head home, so mother can go home. It was great that she spent time with our children, and I will see you at home."

As she left for home she asked, "Peter at what time do you want supper?"

Peter replied, "I'll be home to eat with the family, but remember to visit the new member."

"Okay dear. I will do that before I go home. Love you. bye."

Cindy left to visit the new member of the church, she was a very nice lady. Won't she be glad to have company. Cindy arrived at the door of the new member, and knocked on her door. It was a small place, but very nice. She waited for the door to open, but there was no answer so she knocked again. There was still no answer, so she went home and told Peter she would try later or tomorrow. Lynda was still there when Peter and Cindy got home, and was greeted with a hug from her.

"So glad you could be with the twins, Mother. It was a big help. Thank you. By the way, where are the twins?" Peter asked.

"They're in the back playing with friends." replied Lynda. "They have been little angels. I love those two darlings, we had a good time."

"Why don't you and Geroge stay for supper," asked Peter. "We haven't spent much time together lately."

"That sounds like an invitation I can't turn down," said Lynda. "I will call George at the school and let him know. I think he will like that. He's been so busy at the school, when he gets home he isn't hungry and just sits by the fire!" It seems like he can't get warm enough. I hope he isn't coming down with a cold, but I'm sure he would love to come. Thank you both." Mom said.

Peter said, "I am glad you are here. I thank God every day for you and Dad. I'll never forget when Dad found me on the street. It was the best thing that could have happened to my life, besides Mother Glennis."

Lynda called George and they and the twins had a good visit with Grandpa. Hope said, "listen, Grandpa. I can play all by myself."

She played a tune called Mary had a Little

Lamb. "How was that Grandpa?" she asked.

"That was wonderful, Hope!" George said. "What about Georgie, can you do anything?"

"No Grandpa, I take karate classes!" And he showed them what he could do.

"Good Georgie. Always be careful not to hurt anyone," said Grandpa gave Georgie and Hope a big hug. "I love you two Rascals."

"Well," said Lynda. "I am ready to go home and get a good night's sleep, how about you George?" She asked.

"I am ready honey, it has been a long day at the school. A couple of new boys are coming in tomorrow. Peter do you think you could help for a while tomorrow?"

"Sure Dad I'd be glad to," he said. "What time are they coming?"

"Early morning, Son. 9 a.m."

"I will be there to help Dad, you just get a good nights sleep." Peter hugged his dad and mom and said, "we will see you tomorrow, goodnight."

Hope and Georgie ran and gave them both a hug also. "Bye Grandma and Grandpa."

Peter and the family went back to the house and Cindy gave Hope her milk along with a Jell-O treat. In the evening, they just enjoyed being together reading Bible stories and discussing the things that happened during the day. Hope and Georgie showed Peter and Cindy their collection of leaves and flowers that they picked on their walk with Grandma.

"It was a good day," Peter said.

"Yes," said Cindy. "Except I couldn't get a hold of the new member you asked me to visit. Mrs. Perkins."

"Well we will try tomorrow, okay?" said Peter. "Maybe she was resting."

The next morning, Peter went to help his Dad, and Cindy and the twins went to visit the new member. But there was no response. The door was open, so Cindy called the girl. "Miss Perkins," she called, "this is Cindy Watkins, Peter's wife. Are you here?"

The Twins were in the car while Cindy went in. Cindy looked around was afraid there was something wrong. She walked into the bedroom only to find the young lady had died during the night. She called the police and then took the twins home and called Peter. It was very sad for Cindy as she wished she had gone in the night before to see if she was okay. It made her think of her mother.

"Mommy," said Hope, "what happened? Is Miss Perkins all right."

"Well, Miss Perkins must have had a heart attack last night."

"What is a heart attack?" the twins asked.

Cindy tried to explain to the twins but wasn't sure they understood. "Miss Perkins went to join her Father in heaven, and God will take care of her. So we will keep her in our prayers, okay?"

"How would you like to go visit Grandpa at the school?" asked Cindy.

"We would like that," the twins said. They were so excited, they had forgotten about Miss Perkins, but Cindy's reason was to let Peter and George know.

When they arrived at the school, Cindy found Peter and George in the office and asked to talk to them. "Do you have someone who could show the twins around?" she asked.

"Sure," George said. "Mr. Martin will be glad to do that. I will call him."

While the twins went with him, they asked all kinds of questions and Cindy said to Peter and his dad, "remember the young lady I went to see this morning?"

"Yes, she was to be a new member Sunday,"

said Peter. "Did you get a hold of her?"

"Yes," Cindy replied, "but, but I found her in her bed. She had a heart attack. She was so young, do you have her Mother and Dad's phone number?"

Both men were surprised to hear that Miss Perkins died. "The poor girl. I just met her last week, and she seemed good." said Peter.

"What can we do?" asked George.

"Well if you can find her parents, that would help. I don't know anything about her," Cindy said.

"Okay," the men offered to take care of everything and they took hands and prayed for her. Just when the twins came running in, "Mommy, Daddy, Grandpa! We saw lots of rooms and boys that live here."

Grandpa hugged them both and said, "some day you two will take over in Grandpa's place. Would you like that?"

The twins didn't say anything, they smiled and looked at each other.

"All right kids," said Cindy, "let's go for lunch, and then home okay? Maybe we can stop at the park."

The Twins were all excited and we're ready to go. "Bye Grandpa and Daddy!" they called out.

When Peter was done helping his Dad with the new boys, Billy and Paul, he left for the church to see how he could help Miss Perkins, and if her parents were living. How could this happen to such a young girl, and why did God call her before his membership? He looked at the information Miss Perkins gave him, and made a few phone calls. A man answered the last call and Peter said, "is this the Perkins Family?"

He answered yes and Peter asked if he could come and see them. Mr. Perkins said okay but didn't know why.

"I will explain when I get there. See you soon," and he left to meet Miss Perkins father.

When Peter got to the Perkins' home, he rang the doorbell and a short stocky guy opened the door.

"Hello," Peter said. "I am the pastor from the church that Debbie was going to join on Sunday. Is...is she alright? asked Mr. Perkins.

"Well, maybe you better sit down. Is her mother here?" asked Peter.

"No, what's this about, and where is Debbie? Where is my little girl?" He asked.

"That's what I came to tell you. She passed away last night."

"What did you say? It can't be, she just got her own apartment and didn't say anything about not feeling well."

"Mr. Perkins," said Peter. "If there is anything I can do for you, I'll be glad to help."

Peter gave him the number of a funeral home and the church's phone number to call. Mr. Perkins was feeling weak.

"I will see you tomorrow. You may call or come anytime." Peter asked if he was going to be okay before he left and felt very sad for him. Mr. Perkins came to the church the next day and made arrangements for his daughter. His wife had died two years ago. The service and burial went well. Mr. Perkins met new friends and became a member of the church that his daughter was going to join. The Watkins' stopped and had invited him over for dinner. Mr. Perkins thanked everyone for all their kindness.

The summer had come and gone. Hope had been a sick little girl, but had a lot of rest. She had gotten stronger before school had to start. Peter had to question God's ways, but found they weren't what God had done to Hope, but what he blamed God for. Sometimes we all wonder why things happen, and Peter asked

God to forgive him. George and Lynda enjoyed the grandchildren. It made their summer more exciting. But now it was time to get back to school and Hope was looking forward to it. Georgie was okay, but he just liked to play ball and ride his bike. Hope was in second grade, Georgie was also.

But they were in different classes so they could think for themselves and not depend on each other. At first it was hard for the twins to be separated. Georgie would say, "Dad, why can't I be with Hope in her class. I can only see her at recess."

"Well," Peter said, "the teacher thought it would be good for Hope. She needs a little more care because they have to watch her diet and make sure she eats at certain times. They thought you were a strong little boy. You are, aren't you Georgie? You will see her at recess and come home with her on the bus, so you need to watch over her on the bus. Can you do that?" asked Peter.

"Okay Daddy, we can help each other at home and play."

The Twins were very close. They did everything together with their friends. They have their room together, and the same television programs. But gradually Hope was practicing piano more and more. Was this going to be her choice as she grows older? Soon as the twins got home from school, they did their homework and then outside they went to see their friends. They would play hide and go seek, or ride bikes with them. He would let them play until it started getting dark, and then Peter would come home and grab them both up and carry them in for supper. "Now you little rascals better go wash those busy little hands and faces before supper."

"Okay Daddy," and they would see who could get there first. Such a joy they are.

School time was a time for the family. Georgie had joined soccer again, and Hope took piano lessons after school from the neighbor next door. Hope always enjoyed going over there, even if it was to help them rake leaves or play with her little kittens. She has a dog called Soccer, and loves animals. She sometimes faced the dog, but usually would get sweaty along with Soccer. The growing and learning to take care of pets was good for Hope. It gave her a feeling of helping her Mom and Dad. This made her feel proud. She was doing good in school, she would always have good reports.

Georgie, well he wasn't a role model, but he

was smart but just was all boy. He figured he knew it so he didn't do his work. If the teacher had a mistake on the board when they did craft work, he would tell her it was wrong, and he would help some of the others with the things they were making. He was active and got bored very easily. Peter and Cindy were often called to school to talk to the teachers, but as Georgie settled down he began to enjoy school more. When there were vacation days like Thanksgiving or Christmas, they would go to childcare for the older children with Cindy because she taught Bible School two days a week. The days Peter would make sure he and Cindy would spend time together. George and Hope always make sure they got to see Grandpa and Grandma during the holidays during the time off. For Thanksgiving, Georgie actually spent time by Lynda's and George's, and they told Little Georgie, "you can stay as long as you want with us, and Hope too if it's okay with your Mom."

"Oh boy can we Mom? they asked.

"Well," Cindy looked at Peter and Peter said, "you can spend the night with Grandma and Grandpa, and we will see you all tomorrow in church and Grandma's big turkey dinner."

"Thanks Daddy!" the twins said.

"You remember to be good, and no karate kicking."

So the twins stayed with Lynda and George. Peter and Cindy joined them for Thanksgiving dinner.

"Mom," Peter said, "that was a very good dinner. I hope everyone had a good dinner at the church. We set up tables and turkey dinners for those who had no one to share it with. Mr. Perkins was going to help serve them. He misses his family a lot, but this will give him a piece of mind knowing he could help others!"

"Well I am sure he feels better and closer to God than he did," replied George. "It will be hard for them at Christmas time, with no family."

"Dad, why don't we invite him to spend Christmas day with us?" Peter said.

"That's a great idea Peter, we will wait till closer to Christmas and ask him."

Hope wasn't able to eat the turkey, but she loved the cranberries, corn, and salad. "So I guess she didn't go hungry. How is she doing with her diet?"

"She was doing well. She goes back to the Doctor in a couple of weeks, the protein count has gone down. Praise God." Cindy said.

The next day after Thanksgiving, Peter and Cindy took the twins for a ride to show them where he used to live with his first mom and dad and went to visit the cemetery.

"Daddy," asked Hope, "why are we going here, what are all the big stones over there?"

"Well do you remember when Miss Perkins died and we went to her funeral?"

"Yes," they answered. "But how come we are here?"

This was new to them and why all the stones were out there. Peter and Cindy parked the car and showed the twins by the stones, or as we know them as markers, were all out there.

"Georgie, remember we went by Daddy's old house when his first mom lived there?"

"Yes," said Georgie.

"Well," said Peter. "Can you see the name on this marker, see the name on it?"

"Yes Dad," the twins replied. "Is that your Mom and Dad?"

"Yes sweetie, they are buried here, but their souls are up in heaven with God. It's a beautiful place up there!"

The twins had other questions, like how did

they get here and other questions that young children would ask at that age. Peter told them they would understand when they were a little older. Cindy and Peter put fresh flowers on the graves and went riding to see more sights before they went home.

Peter stopped at the church to pick up some paperwork. The next couple of days he prepared his sermon, and Cindy occupied her time with the twins. Georgie had come down with a cold so he didn't feel like going anywhere. Peter stayed with him, also Cindy took Hope to the store, her first field trip alone with her mom. They were looking at toys, clothes, and other things that caught their eyes. It was a nice mother-daughter time together. When Monday came the normal routine started, but Georgie still wasn't feeling well. So they took him to the Doctor and he gave Georgie some medicine and told him to stay in bed and keep warm until he felt better. It was two or three days before Georgie started feeling better. He started eating more and laughing.

"I am so glad you are better Georgie," said Hope because she couldn't go see him while he had a fever." Now you can play with me."

They got some of their games out on the TV

like Nintendo games. Peter and Cindy were glad to see them playing and Georgie feeling better. The family was back to normal and it was so great.

Christmas time was exciting for the twins. All the decorations on the streets, homes, and the yards were all decorated. The twins were anxious for Santa to come. Christmas programs were even on the way in church and school for the twins. Hope's teacher had asked her if she would like to play a song on the piano at the Christmas program. "Will you ask your mother, Hope?" asked the teacher. "I will send a note also."

"I will ask Mommy," said Hope. "What song can I play?"

"You can play any song, especially a Christmas song. Maybe your piano teacher can help you," replied the teacher.

Hope practiced every day on the piano. Georgie was still going to be in a play at school. He wasn't too happy about being on the stage, Peter and him practiced his part all night. They both did well on their parts, and sang with the rest of the school class. A week later, Hope played this song for church program and sang Christmas songs together. She was doing well as a second grader on the piano. Peter and Cindy were so proud of her, and her grandparents were also. The following Sunday before Christmas, Peter took the Sunday school children on a sleigh ride singing Christmas carols at shut-in houses. Even George and Lynda went with them and enjoyed every bit of it. The beautiful trees and lights and children laughing. That was the most beautiful sound of all.

That week, the twins were on vacation time. "No school!" said Georgie, "yeah!"

They could play in the snow. Dad could take some ice skating. Georgie didn't mind the snow or the cold. They enjoyed shopping and looking for a present for Peter, and Grandpa, and Grandma Watkins with Cindy. George was walking ahead of her and saw a man in a red and white suit, "Mommy, Mommy, look at Santa Claus. Can we go see him! Can we mommy?" asked George.

She said, "okay let's go, but be patient and polite because there is a lot of other children waiting to see him in the line."

Finally, the twins sat on Santa's lap and told him what they wanted for Christmas. Cindy was ready to go home and the twins were hungry, so they stopped for lunch and then at the church to see Peter, who was busy planning his Sunday Services.

"Daddy," Hope ran to him. "We saw Santa Claus, he's bringing me a big doll for Christmas."

"What did you ask Santa for Georgie?"

"Well I told him I would like a train set."

"Well," Peter said, "Santa has a lot of children to deliver to, but I'm sure he will make it here if you are very good little children!"

"Okay!"

They all went home together and Peter spent time with the twins while Cindy got the preparations done for Christmas dinner. She had called Lynda and George to see what time they could come for Christmas dinner, because George and Lynda had to stop at the school first to wish the boys a Merry Christmas.

The next few days were busy ones for Peter delivering gifts to the shut-ins. He had called his father to help him, and George was more than happy to help. They visited the hospitals and then last of all to the prisoners who couldn't go home for Christmas. Peter said to George, "Well I guess that just about does it for this year."

"I suppose your family is all excited for tomorrow. So you better get home and spend time with them son."

"Oh Dad," said Peter. "Did you call Mr. Perkins and ask him to dinner?"

"Yes Son we will pick him up on our way to your house. He is looking forward to it."

"Thanks Dad, we will see you and Mom tomorrow and Mr. Perkins." They both went home to their families.

When Peter returned home, he told Cindy all of the places he had been with George and what a joy it was to see the smiles on the faces and how grateful the prisoners were to receive a Christmas gift. "Dad and I stopped at the school, also Jerry and John were there visiting. They are doing great and it was nice to see them with the other boys singing and laughing. They really turned out to be good boys. Praise God," said Peter.

As the evening quieted down, the family gathered around the Christmas tree and Peter told them the story of when he was a little boy and how his mother never had much money and lived in a small house in Rome, Georgia. He told them how his father worked in the coal mines and died at a young age. His mother cleaned homes, scrubbed floors.

"My mother, Mrs. Glennis, went and sold bread

to other neighbors in stores. She later died of pneumonia. She was a wonderful mother. I was only twelve years old."

"What did you do Daddy?" Hope asked, "where did you go? Were you all alone?"

"Well I walked the streets looking for work and food. It was cold and dark. I was so tired I collapsed on the street, and do you know what happened after that?"

"No Daddy, what happened?" The twins very curiously asked him.

"Well your Grandpa came along that night and took me to the hospital, and then took me home to be his little boy. So you see, when Jesus was born, God sent a star for the wise men to follow to the stable. So this, my little ones, was a blessing from God to have parents like your Grandma and Grandpa who adopted me and loved me very much. And I love them very much."

"I love them too, Daddy," said Georgie.

"Well it is time to get ready for bed, and get some sleep if you want Santa to come," replied Cindy. "Let's go, we will be in to hear your prayers." They crawled into bed.

"Okay Daddy, we're ready." Peter and Cindy

went in and listened to their prayers, and kissed them goodnight.

Christmas day arrived with little feet on the stairs, faces aglow as they ran into Peter's room. "Mommy, Daddy come on Santa came!"

"We are coming," said Cindy as they crawled out of bed and went downstairs. "I guess we have to wait for Grandpa and Grandma."

"Why Mommy? We want to open one, can we?" asked Georgie.

Hope's eyes were so bright at seeing all the gifts Santa brought, that she just looked at it all. They opened one gift each and then waited for their grandparents. George and Lynda arrived with Mr. Perkins and took the twins outside so they didn't see them come in with the gifts. Then they all gathered around the tree and opened their gifts. Mr. Perkins was surprised there was something for him too. After opening presents, they joined around the table and gave thanks to the Lord and then sat down to dinner.

"Remember last year," said George, "how nice it was when Jerry and John came for the holidays and had dinner with us? Well this year we have a new friend, and we are very happy to have him with us. He has been a lot of help!"

Mr. Perkins was very honored to be part of their friends and family. Peter got up and walked to the window. "Look everyone, look at the star. The one that's really bright."

"That looks like a star I saw when I found you on the street Peter," said George. "It was a beautiful bright star. It must have led us to you Son! I thank God."

"And so do I," said Lynda.

The children were playing so hard all day that they fell asleep next to the toys under the tree. "Guess it is time to call it a day," George replied. "Lynda and I will take Mr. Perkins home while you get the twins in bed okay?"

Mr. Perkins thanked Peter and Cindy for a wonderful time and dinner. "Merry Christmas to you all," he replied.

George wished them a Merry Christmas, and he and Lynda left and took their guest home.

When Lynda got home she was tired and happy all in one. "What would it be like without Peter and his family George?"

"I'm just glad we don't have to find out!"

George and Lynda sat in front of the fire and thanked each other for the gift. The next morning it was snowing, how beautiful it looked. The sun was shining on the snow. "It is just a beautiful picture that God paints for us," said Lynda. "This has been a beautiful Christmas."

The following week the children were back in school. A new year started. Peter was busy at church greeting a few new members and teaching them the ways of God, and Cindy was to complete her Discipleship classes and be ordained into her Ministry. The twins were doing good in school, even Georgie!

A few years passed and Hope had become a piano player and played in concerts and worked different places after she graduated. Georgie went on to college to become a sports man or a soccer coach, to work with his Grandpa at the Christian School. Georgie likes working with his Grandpa, he was very good with the younger boys that were alone and unhappy. He could always get them to laugh.

When Hope was playing at concerts, they would all make sure they went to listen to her play even, Little Georgie told her she was very good. That made Hope smile and gave him a big hug and said, "thanks brother."

They didn't see each other except on the weekends when everyone was home. Sometimes

Hope had to be gone on the weekends, that made it very quiet and lonesome for Cindy and Peter. Georgie missed her when she wasn't there, but he would help with other things at the church, like doing things on the computer. He would help the boys at the school and teach them to play soccer. They became quite good at it. Georgie became a coach in Rome, the little town he was raised in, and when he worked at the boys school he taught the younger boys how to play and be honest and fair to each other as friends, and how to help and be kind to each other. He became very fond of the boys and began teaching to play football.

He became very good in Rome, and Peter was very proud of his son. He was hoping Georgie would follow him and Ministry, but knew he couldn't force Georgie to be like him. But was happy he was working with the boys and his dad.

George and Lynda had gone on vacation to Florida where it was warmer, because George hadn't been very well. He had gotten quite sick while they were gone and had to fly home. Peter was there to meet them and rushed him to the hospital. "What's wrong dad? You're going to be okay," Peter said.

When they got him to the hospital, they had called Hope and let her know how sick her Grandpa was. She rushed home as soon as her concert was over. She went to the hospital where the rest of the family was waiting for the doctor's report. She wanted to see him right away.

"Dad please, I have to see him!"

"Okay come on. I will let you see him but be very quiet."

The nurse was by his side and said it was okay, but not too long. They all went in by George's side and prayed for him to get well. Cindy was with Lynda, who was crying and hoping her husband would be fine.

Georgie said, "grandpa I need you at the school! Please get well. I...I will keep the school running for you grandpa." Georgie started crying.

"I love you Grandpa," said Hope.

They both laid their heads on George, and Peter and Cindy said, "children let Grandpa rest, I will come out in a minute."

Cindy took them out so Peter and his mom could be alone for a while with his dad. They knew it was almost that time for the angels to come for him, and they both shed tears together as the nurse said to them, "he has gone."

"Lynda I'm sorry."

Peter and his mother stayed in the room for a while and the rest of the family went back in to say their goodbyes to their special person in their lives. When everything was over, there was an empty feeling in their hearts. Peter knew that empty feeling was because he had gone through it before when he lost his parents. He wondered what his Mother would do now that his Dad was gone. How will the twins take it not seeing Grandpa anymore?

When the funeral was over, the twins missed him very much and Lynda. Well Peter and Cindy kept her at their house until she was able to be alone. The people in Peter's church gave their respects to the family by bringing food and just being there to talk. George Jr stayed at the school as he promised his Grandpa. In time, Lynda went to take care of the school and help Georgie with the other boys. She also hired another helper to support little George so George could coach again, and the boys were glad to have him back.

Cindy thought of her Mom at this time and wished God had given her more time to spend with her and the twins. She accepted the fact that only God has the answers. He had given them two wonderful children, a Christian husband, and a mother-in-law whom she loved as much as her own Mother. Peter's Mom was her Mother also.

Peter missed his Father Watkins very much. He missed talking and doing things together as a young boy. But now he had to focus on Mother Watkins in the family God gave him. Eventually, Lynda moved in with Peter and the family. She was becoming too old to live alone. Whenever Hope and Georgie were home, one or the other would go for a walk with her and show her some places around the town that had changed. She enjoyed their company and they enjoyed doing things for her. She was their special Grandma, just like Grandpa was their special Grandpa.

Hope went on to teach music to other children, and her diet for her health condition was a thing she had conquered and she was satisfied with her life. But kept seeing her doctor on a regular basis, as he told her she would have to.

Cindy worked at the church when she could, but taking care of Mother Watkins was her priority, and Peter appreciated that. Peter still thought about his Mom and Dad Glennis. He and Lynda would go to the cemetery to visit his Dad and to see his paternal parents, along with Cindy's mom. He only wished the twins had known Grandma and Grandpa Glennis. They both thanked God for the blessings he gave them - love, family, and faith. What more could anyone ask out of life?

They had a good life together, and God had given him his church, and a home to raise his family. As George Watkins had given him a home like his mother Glennis said he would. Her prayers had come true.

The End.

About the Author

I was born in Wisconsin in 1932 and placed in an orphanage for 3 years. I then moved to a farm where I grew up and enjoyed all the animals. I loved feeding them and walking in the fields.

My great-grandfather was the founder of the famous Pillsbury Mills in Minnesota in the 1800's. After graduating from Waupaca High School, I moved to the town of Waukesha, WI. I married in 1954 and have three birth children, and adopted a baby girl who is as precious as my birth ones. Her name is Karen.

I love going for walks and helping other people. I enjoy the Joy Circle Group at church and have been a member of the First United Methodist Church since 1957. In Waukesha, WI, writing my book, A Father's Love, has made my faith in God strong enough to get through life a lot easier.

www.ingramcontent.com/pod-product-compliance
Lightning Source LLC
Chambersburg PA
CBHW071215090426
42736CB00014B/2833